# Solo-preneuring

## THE ART OF EARNING A LIVING WITHOUT A JOB

## Cathy Stucker

Special Interests Publishing
SUGAR LAND, TEXAS

Cathy Stucker may be contacted via e-mail at: cathy@idealady.com.
Special Interests Publishing
www.sipub.com

Book Layout © BookDesignTemplates.com
Solo-preneuring / Cathy Stucker. — 5th ed.
ISBN 978-1-888983-56-2

# Contents

YOUR WORK IS GOING TO FILL
A LARGE PART OF YOUR LIFE,
AND THE ONLY WAY TO
•••••••••••••••••••••••••••••••••
BE TRULY SATISFIED
IS TO DO WHAT YOU
BELIEVE IS GREAT WORK.
●  ● THE ONLY WAY
TO DO GREAT
WORK IS TO LOVE
WHAT YOU DO.
-STEVE JOBS

# CHAPTER 1

# Solo-preneuring: Integrating Your Work and Your Life

Do you love your job? Do you look forward to going to work every day? Do you enjoy your work so much that you can't imagine doing anything else? Or have you noticed that Monday through Friday the clocks seem to run a lot slower than they do on the weekends?

Most people drag themselves to an office, factory or store day after day, living for the weekends and vacations when they can enjoy life. Or waiting for retirement, when they will travel, take time for hobbies, or maybe start a new career doing what they always wanted to do. Work is something they have to do, and it seems that everything else in their lives has to be fit in around it. Even the word "work" has a negative association for most people.

The reason you feel so tired at the end of your workday has a lot more to do with your mental attitude than with the work. When you are doing work you don't enjoy it drains your energy and joy. Have you ever noticed the difference in how you feel after a day of working hard at something you love, rather than something you "have to do"? Even if you are physically tired, it's a good feeling. A feeling of accomplishment. Sleep comes easily, and it is a restful sleep that recharges you and prepares you for the next day.

A day spent doing work you don't enjoy leaves you tired and emotionally drained. You fall into bed exhausted, but you don't sleep peacefully. You may even have anxious dreams about work left undone, or what you will face the next day.

Imagine waking up in the morning excited and happy about each new day. And doing work that is so in tune with your talents and interests, that it hardly seems like work to you. That's what Solo-preneurs do.

Solo-preneurs create their own careers. They aren't tied to one occupation, and they set their own priorities. Your chosen path will not be the same as anyone else's, because it will reflect your choices.

Solo-preneuring is a form of self-employment, but it is much more. It enables you to integrate your work and your life so that you feel good about what you do for a living.

**Solo-preneuring is getting paid for**

**doing what you love.**

**It is taking control of your work and your life.**

As you read this book and work the exercises in the accompanying workbook you will discover the possibilities that exist for the Solo-preneur. Ideas will pop in to your head as you read, so make lots of notes throughout the book. Don't count on remembering that brilliant thought. Write it down!

I've provided some guidelines for deciding what you want to do, getting started, meeting legal and tax requirements, marketing, and more. But the most important thing to remember is that there are no rules about being a Solo-preneur. As a Solo-preneur you control your own destiny.

Ask yourself what you would do if there were no limits. How would you spend your time, where would you go? Then set about removing the limits you have imposed on yourself (I can't ..., I could never ..., I've never been able to ..., etc.) and start living your dreams.

Good luck in your adventure!

*Cathy*

P.S. Be sure to download the free workbook to help you get started in making your dream career happen. Go to https://IdeaLady.com/workbook

# CHAPTER 2

# What is "Solo-preneuring"?

Most people believe that you have only two choices: you can be an employee of someone else, or you can start a business and have others working for you.

As an employee, you have to perform up to the expectations of others: your bosses. That means working the hours they set, doing the work they give you, in the way they tell you to do it. In exchange, you get the security of a regular paycheck and benefits. Of course, we've all seen in the last several years that there is nothing secure about anyone's paycheck.

Entrepreneurs work on their terms, but that doesn't mean they have it easy. Launching a business requires a commitment of time and money, and may take all of both that the entrepreneur can scrape together. Often, the entrepreneur has not gone from slave to master, but has merely traded one master (the boss) for another (the business).

That brings us to an alternative: the Solo-preneur. The Solo-preneur chooses the work he wants to do. She decides how much or how little to work. He is not faced with the pressures of having to make a payroll, nor is he faced with the prospect of dragging himself to an office, day after day, to do the same old job. Most importantly, the Solo-preneur controls her own destiny. No one person can decide that the Solo-preneur will lose her livelihood.

In short, the Solo-preneur can have the best of both worlds: freedom from corporate bondage, without taking on the shackles of responsibility required to run a business. How, then, does the Solo-preneur make a living? By finding ways to turn his interests into profit centers. A profit center is any way of making money. You are not limited to one profit center; in fact, most Solo-preneurs have several, each bringing in a portion of their total income. We will talk about how you can establish multiple profit centers in a later chapter.

The Solo-preneur finds ways to make money doing the things he enjoys, while minimizing or eliminating the aspects of work he doesn't want to do. An accountant may enjoy working with numbers, but is tired of the long hours and commuting of her present job. She could choose to start an accounting practice from her home and work only the hours she wishes, or she could spend part of her time doing accounting (perhaps working part time for her present employer, maybe even telecommuting), and part of her time developing a new profit center based on another hobby or interest.

Solo-preneurs may choose to earn all of their money through self-employment, or they may choose to have a part-time job or do contract or temp work in addition to starting one or more business ventures.

It's important to remember that there aren't a lot of rules about becoming a Solo-preneur. However, there are laws and regulations about small businesses. Although you won't operate like a traditional entrepreneur, you are still subject to the laws imposed on business, so be sure you know what those laws are and abide by them. You will see more about this later in the book.

The key to Solo-preneuring is flexibility. Your enterprise can be as big or as little as you wish. You may start out small and grow to a large enterprise employing many others, or you may keep it small enough that you remain the only "employee." You can pursue it full-time or part-time, or even in your spare time for extra income while you remain employed.

As a Solo-preneur, you may choose to do only one type of work. Or, you may combine two or more related functions, such as being an organizer and a virtual assistant. You may even combine two or more completely unrelated pursuits.

My personal experience illustrates what is possible. I worked in the insurance industry for about 15 years. In early 1994, I saw the unmistakable signs that my job was going to be eliminated within 6 months to a year.

When you are an employee and see your job is in danger, your first thought is that you have to find another job. I put a resume together and went on some interviews, and decided very quickly that I did not want another job. But I didn't think I wanted to start a business, either. And I wasn't sure that the businesses in which I was interested would generate the work (and the income) I needed as quickly as I needed them to.

I started developing a fantasy about what my perfect job would be. After mulling it over for a few weeks, I realized that I could make my fantasy a reality. Instead of expecting my income to come from one job or one business, I could do several different things, each of which would provide a part of my income.

Now I had a plan. I started implementing my plan, and I actually started looking forward to getting laid off. When it finally happened on October 31, 1994, I was ready to hit the ground running.

That original plan has changed and evolved over the years, as new opportunities presented themselves, and I moved on from some of the things I had been doing. I can do anything that interests and challenges me, take on new roles, and shed the ones that no longer fit. New technology has changed the way much of my business is conducted.

So far, I have earned income by presenting seminars which I sponsored, or were sponsored by colleges, industry associations and other organizations, and as a contract seminar presenter for an international public seminar company. I have sold insurance, and conducted insurance enrollments as a contractor for insurance companies as well as through my own enrollment company. I've consulted in person and by phone with Solo-preneurs and small businesses all over the U.S. and in Canada. I've written and published a number of manuals, workbooks, booklets, ebooks, reports and other information products which I sell through seminars and speaking engagements, through bookstores and online booksellers, by mail order, through my own website, and through others. I get paid to shop and eat as a mystery shopper, and I've even been a movie extra.

Don't be overwhelmed by that list. I didn't do all of them at the same time. And you don't have to develop a list as long as mine. The things I have done as a Solo-preneur have all come naturally, based on my interests and the opportunities I saw before me.

The biggest changes in my business have happened because of the Internet. There are so many ways to make money, starting with little or no money, that have been made possible by the Internet.

What has remained constant throughout my journey is that I control my own destiny. I decide which opportunities to pursue and which to let go. I decide how many hours I want to work. Ultimately, the choices I make are about the life I want to live, and how my work fits into that life.

As you go through this book and the exercises in the workbook, you will see how you can create your own perfect job as a Solo-preneur. Use your imagination and forget the old rules about how you are "supposed" to make money. This is a new age, and there are new possibilities.

Work doesn't have to be drudgery. It can be enjoyable. And your life doesn't have to be something you fit in around your work. Solo-preneurs mesh their work and their lives together, because they get satisfaction and other personal rewards from their work, not just money from doing a job.

Solo-preneurs can earn money through:
- a part-time or full-time job
- contract or temporary work
- direct sales
- one or more businesses they start and run
- investments
- any combination of the above.

There has never been a better time to be a Solo-preneur and create the life and work of your dreams!

# I THINK THE
## *foremost quality* –
### THERE'S NO SUCCESS
# WITHOUT IT -

---

**IS REALLY LOVING WHAT YOU DO.**

## *If you love it,*
## *you do it well,*
**AND THERE'S NO SUCCESS IF
YOU DON'T DO WELL WHAT**
## YOU'RE WORKING AT.

— *Malcolm Forbes* —

# Can I Really Support Myself This Way?

Yes, you certainly can. Many people do. I do, and you can, too. The secret to success is starting small (without a lot of upfront expense) and adding new profit centers to build your income.

Before you can succeed, though, you have to believe that you can. The exercises in the downloadable workbook can help you to see the possibilities and develop the plan that will get you from where you are today to where you want to be.

## Do You Have What it Takes?

Virtually anyone can be a Solo-preneur. Here are the requirements:

**Curiosity and creativity** - Solo-preneurs are open to new ideas and they are willing to look at things in a different way. They like to ask "Why?" but more often they ask "Why not?"

**Self-discipline** - There won't be a boss standing over you making you work, so you have to motivate yourself. While you will choose work you care about and enjoy, there will be tasks (maybe balancing your checkbook) that you don't enjoy but have to do.

**Basic money skills** - You don't have to be a financial wizard, but it is important to understand your expenses, manage your cash flow, and keep an eye on the bottom line.

**Time management skills** - Because the Solo-preneur may have several projects going at once, she must be able to organize and prioritize each task to make sure the most important tasks are done first, and all are done timely.

**An interest in something and a way to make money with it** - Most of us can easily identify our interests, so the next step is to determine how to make money with them. This book and the exercises in the workbook will help you to find ways to turn your passions into cash.

---

## What Can You Do?

You have skills and abilities that others do not. We often undervalue the things we know and what we can do, thinking, "If I can do it, anyone can." Well, "anyone" can't. Maybe you are an excellent cook, or a Civil War buff, or you know all about computers. Whatever your knowledge or skills, they are of value to others. All you have to do is figure out how to package and market them.

One example of this is the book you're reading now. When I was faced with losing my job, I spent a lot of time thinking about what I wanted to do and re-searching my options. In no time at all I figured out that I did not want to get another job, but it took me a while longer to figure out how I could earn my liv-ing without one.

When I thought about teaching others how to be Solo-preneurs, it seemed to me that no one would pay for information like this. "It's so obvious," I thought. Wrong! It was obvious to me how to earn a living without a job because I spent months researching ways to earn money, government regulations and taxes, and the other issues covered in this book before launching my Solo-preneuring ventures. People who don't want to spend months reinventing the wheel can benefit from this information.

There are lots of ways to earn money as a Solo-preneur. Some of the business models that work well include:

- Make something
- Sell Something
- Write something
- Teach something
- Do something

You may not immediately see how to turn your interest into a profit center, but try looking at it from a different perspective. If you know how to make the world's best cheesecakes, one option would be to bake and sell your cheesecakes. But how else could you use that skill to generate income? You could write and self-publish a cookbook of cheesecake recipes. Or you could teach a class on making the perfect cheesecake. There are probably many other ways that you could think of once you open your mind to the possibilities.

Start looking for things you can do to make money. You may think that you don't have any ideas, and maybe you don't have ideas today. However, when you start paying attention and looking, things turn up all over the place.

One day radio host Dave Ramsey was talking with a listener who had gotten out of debt using Dave's Financial Peace program. The listener had started a side business repairing and selling furniture. He found that a lot of people were giving away furniture on CraigsList. Generally, it was broken or damaged in some way, but most of it only required minor repair. He would pick up the furniture, make the repair, then turn around and sell it. Where did he sell it? On CraigsList, of course!

That sounds like it could be a good way to make a few extra bucks, right? Well, in one year, this guy made 24,000 "extra" bucks repairing and selling furniture he got free. And he did this in his spare time, while he was working a full-time job.

I am not telling you to start picking up broken furniture so you can repair it and sell it. That might not be your thing. Odds are, it's not. But what can you do? Start looking and you will find ideas everywhere.

Some examples of the types of work perfectly suited to Solo-preneuring are:

- Consulting
- Computer and Internet Businesses
- Teaching and Seminar Leading
- Crafts
- Personal Services
- Business Services
- Entertainment
- Swap Meet or Craft Fair Vendor
- Contract Work/Temping
- Writing

Just about anything you can do can become a Solo-preneur venture. The workbook includes exercises to help you pinpoint your interests and turn them into moneymakers. Be open-minded and creative.

## ASK YOURSELF:

**What do I know that others don't?**

**What can I do that others can't?**

**What will I do that others won't?**

**What can I do for others faster, cheaper, better**

**than they can do it for themselves?**

# CHAPTER 4

# The Gig Economy

The "gig economy" is getting a lot of attention these days, both positive and negative. If you are not familiar with the idea, the Macmillan Dictionary defines it as, "an employment concept in which people are paid for each specific, short-term task that they do and don't have conventional contracts of employment."

Although being forced into the gig economy by the inability to get a full-time job is a bad thing, the gig economy can be a part of your Solo-preneuring strategy, and that is a good thing. It is all about choice.

So what do people do in the gig economy? Just about anything! There are many online sites and apps that connect workers with customers. Choose the ones you want to use, then when you want some work, just see what is available.

Some of the kinds of gigs you can find include:
- Driving gigs, such as Uber and Lyft.
- Home rentals, such as AirBnB.
- Miscellaneous tasks on sites such as TaskRabbit.
- Freelance design, programming and other work on sites such as UpWork.
- Delivery jobs, such as Doordash and Instacart.
- Child care, senior care, petsitting and house-keeping jobs on sites such as Care.com.
- Telecommuting jobs on VirtualVocations.com.

There are many other specialized sites for people looking for work in a particular field or in unusual situations. For example, Workamper.com connects full-time RVers with work opportunities.

To find more opportunities that are a good fit for you, do an online search for terms such as "gig economy jobs" or include terms specific to your situation, such as "senior" or a type of work (e.g., accounting).

# CHAPTER 5

# Selling Your Services

Typically the fastest way to start making money is to sell a service. You probably won't need a long lead time and you won't have to wait for something to be produced. There are all kinds of services, from cleaning houses and mowing lawns to helping people with computer problems to whatever it is that you can do. Just decide what you are going to do for people, find some people who need that service, do it and get paid. It really can be (almost) that simple.

First, determine if you need a license. Check with your local and state governments to see if there is a licensing requirement for the service you are planning to provide. For example, massage therapists typically require a license, but some types of holistic practitioners may not be licensed. You may not need a license to clean homes and offices but, because you will working on someone else's property it would be a good idea to be bonded or insured. Check with your insurance agent about how to do this.

Although you may decide to use a business name, as you get started it is probably not necessary. Just do business under your own name. Once you decide on a business name you can register it (if required in your city, county or state), set up a bank account in that name, and register the .com for your website.

Get business cards made and spread them around. Business cards are an inexpensive form of advertising.

Read the section on pricing to get an idea of what to charge for your services.

---

## Creating and Maintaining Credibility

You are an expert on your topic if you know more about it than most people. I tell my clients to stop thinking of an expert as the person who knows more about something than anyone else in the world. Instead, an expert is the person who knows more about something than anyone else in the *room*. That is my way of saying that if you know more than the average person about something, you are an expert.

Chances are, there is at least one topic on which you are already an expert. But how do you demonstrate to customers that you are someone whom they should trust and learn from?

You may have formal credentials that identify you as an expert. These may include college degrees, licenses, certifications, and other recognized training. In a previous life, I worked in the insurance industry and I have a bunch of professional designations. When I handed someone a card that had CEBS, CLU, FLMI and an alphabet soup of other credentials after my name, they were impressed that I had earned those designations. Do you have impressive educational or professional credentials?

You should have direct experience in your area of expertise. It is not enough to have read a book or two on how to do it. Have you done it? What kind of results did you achieve? Have you been able to duplicate those results, perhaps in other markets or by helping clients to have success?

Document your results as specifically as possible. Did you sell a million of something, or six million dollars worth of something? Include numbers and time frames: "I added 40,000 people to my mailing list in one year."

List the clients for whom you have worked. Have you had a lot of clients? Are there some impressive names on your client list? Everyone thinks that their situation is unique, so showing that you have helped people or companies like them will give them confidence in you.

Show testimonials from clients. Testimonials should be specific, describing the benefits they got from working with you. Numbers are good here, too. "Steve showed our sales staff how to close more sales. Their closing percentage increased 150%, and so did our revenues." Include identifying information, such as name, title and company, when possible.

Are you still actively involved in your industry, or are you just teaching it? Let customers know that you are up-to-date by showing current involvement. Are you still in private practice, seeing clients? Are you involved in the day-to-day operations of your business?

Your experience does not have to be in business. Your life experience may be relevant to establishing your credentials. What in your personal history gives you credibility? You may not be a doctor, but if you managed to lose 150 pounds, you can help others to lose weight, too. (Note: If you are presenting something related to health and you do not have medical credentials, it can be useful to get an endorsement from someone who does have formal credentials, such as a doctor or nutritionist. And definitely get them to review your material.)

And, one way to become an expert is to write a book. Not only are authors viewed as experts, the process of writing the book can in itself make you an expert. Being the author of a book conveys instant authority and establishes you as an expert on your topic.

# THE QUESTION
# ISN'T WHO
# IS GOING
## TO LET ME; IT'S
## WHO IS GOING
## TO STOP ME.
### -AYN RAND

# CHAPTER 6

# Make Money with Amazon.com

There are so many different ways to make money with Amazon, that they have an entire section of their website devoted to showing you how to profit with them. Just go to Amazon.com and scroll down toward the bottom of the page. You will see a section that says, "Make Money with Us." Some of the ways you can make money with Amazon include:

Sell on Amazon

Sell Your Services on Amazon

Sell on Amazon Business

Sell Your Apps on Amazon

Become an Affiliate

Advertise Your Products

Self-Publish with Us

Become an Amazon Vendor

The terms and conditions of these programs change from time to time, new programs are added and some programs may be terminated. The fact is, though, that Amazon offers a lot of opportunities for small and micro-businesses to make money online.

I have been selling books and other products on Amazon since 2000 via Amazon Advantage, their program for small publishers. I have sold thousands of books on Amazon Advantage, and it helped me to reach an audience I never could have reached on my own.

Advantage is a great program if you have books and other media products already produced; however, you can also sell via their Print on Demand supplier, CreateSpace.com. With CreateSpace, you do not have to print and ship books anywhere. Just upload your files and when someone makes a purchase, CreateSpace will print and mail the book to them. Then they send you a royalty based on the retail price you set and the cost of producing the book.

Full details are available at the CreateSpace.com website. There is no cost to add your book to CreateSpace, although it is recommended that you buy a copy of the book (a "proof") to check before you put the book into production. The cost for the book and shipping will probably be $5 - $10.

Want to sell ebooks? Amazon's Kindle marketplace is the best place to do that. You get a royalty ranging from 35% to 70% of the retail price you set. There is no cost to publish to Kindle. There are authors making tens of thousands of dollars every month with Kindle. They are not the norm, but lots of other authors are making hundreds or thousands of dollars. As with other Amazon programs, the terms and conditions change from time to time. To learn about publishing to the Kindle platform, go to kdp.amazon.com.

## Beyond Books

You probably know that Amazon sells a lot more than books. Many of the products you see on Amazon are not actually sold by Amazon. Just about anyone can list and sell products via the Amazon Marketplace. You can buy just about anything you can imagine on Amazon, and that means that people are selling just about anything you can imagine (and probably quite a few things you can't imagine!)

Initially, Marketplace sellers were responsible for shipping items to customers when they sold. However, now many Marketplace sellers use a program called Fulfillment by Amazon (FBA). With FBA, the seller ships a supply of product to Amazon. When something sells, Amazon ships it to the customer. The seller is not responsible for dealing with the individual orders.

There are still some Marketplace sellers that ship their own orders, but many have shifted to FBA because it is easier, and because it helps them to make sales. When Amazon ships the order, there is no separate shipping charge and customers who are members of Amazon Prime may have the item in just two days. Customers love fast, reliable shipping, so merchants using FBA have a definite advantage. Amazon will even hold and ship inventory you sell elsewhere, so they can be a true fulfillment center for you. Of course, there is a cost for this service, but there is a cost for fulfillment however you do it, even if you do it all yourself.

Thousands of people have created businesses where they buy products wholesale (often importing them from China) then brand them and sell them on Amazon using FBA. If you find a product that is a winner, it can be profitable. However, because a lot of vendors are all sourcing in the same places, many of these products have become commodities that are engaged in a race to the bottom, price-wise. Find something unique, ideally something that is hard for others to source or produce to have the greatest success with this idea.

# IF PLAN A FAILS,

*remember*

## THERE ARE

## 25 MORE

*letters.*

— *Chris Guillebeau* —

# CHAPTER 7

# Selling on eBay

Unless you've been living under a rock, you've heard about eBay over the years. Some people seem to strike it rich on the auction giant's website while others complain that they can't sell anything. So what is the secret to success when it comes to selling on eBay? The first place you have to start is with what kind of products you're actually selling.

Of course, not everyone can sell the same product. Saying that this product or that product will be the key to your success is impossible. However, success does leave clues. You can actually look to see what other people are selling to give yourself an idea about the kinds of products that you can make money from on eBay.

First, you have to decide whether you want to sell used items or new items. In order to sell new items, you would have to find some channel of inventory. You could buy brand-new items at your local retail store or even buy items through a wholesaler. The markup on brand-new items tends to be quite low, so typically sellers make it up in volume. It can also be a bit of a dangerous game because it usually requires more of a monetary investment up front without any assurance that you're going to sell the items.

The way that most people start is by buying items at garage sales and thrift stores, or even by finding items around the house to sell. This is a great way to get started because your investment is low. Items that tend to sell well on eBay include clothing, collectibles, dinnerware, electronics, video games and even shoes. There are hundreds of different categories that you can sell in, so it's impossible to give an exhaustive list. Know your category. Make sure you can tell a real collectible from a fake, and that you know the values of the items you are thinking about buying for resale.

Be careful if you are buying items to resell on eBay. Unless you know your products and your market well, you can end up with a garage full of unsellable junk. A good way to get your feet wet on eBay is to start with stuff you have around the house. Clear out your closets and sell the things you no longer want as a way to get started and learn your way around.

One great way to find out what products are selling on eBay is by using a section of their site called Pulse. If you go to http://pulse.ebay.com, you will be able to look through the categories to see which products have the most bids on them and the most watchers. You can dig down into individual categories to get an idea of what's popular. If you can find some of these items that have the most bids on them, you'll have a sure source of buyers as soon as you list yours.

Selling on eBay can be quite a lucrative venture if you take your time and understand that you will have some failures along the way. Some things simply won't sell, so it's best to get in with little to no investment in the beginning until you get your feet wet and understand the process better.

## Tips For Selling On Ebay

Since its inception in 1995, Ebay has grown on a global scale, selling millions of items each and every month. While having that kind of massive exposure is great for selling a product it also poses a very big, very real problem: how to get customers to buy from you instead of someone else. Knowing specific tips on how to sell on ebay can make all the difference. Here are just a few:

1. Know your product. The more knowledgeable you are about an item, the better you can identify it and describe it to others. Being specific sells.

2. Pictures can determine whether or not your item sells. A potential buyer can only go off of what you are showing them to determine if it is something they want to purchase. If you take bad pictures, you fail to persuade them to buy.

3. Use as many pictures as you need to showcase your item effectively. Sometimes an additional picture will sell an item.

4. Tell as much as you can. You can't give too much information. Buyers are not only looking for key

items, but they are also looking for key words or phrases. Know how to describe a product.

5. Capture them with your title. This is crucial. It determines whether a buyer will open up your listing. A good way to increase your odds of your listing being read is to look at past auctions for similar items that have sold. Take a lesson from their listing and use their wording, as long as it applies.

6. Be reasonable with your price. Just because you believe an item is worth "x" amount of dollars doesn't make it worth that to a buyer. Do your research to determine what your item has been selling for so you don't risk pricing yourself out of the market.

7. Let auctions run long enough to gather attention. Buyers aren't always going to be online when you want them to be. Timing is everything. If your product isn't available when they happen to be looking for it, then it won't sell. Run your auctions long enough to gather sufficient attention. (I like seven days for most items.)

8. End auctions on weekends. (I like to end mine on Sunday evenings.) Many people do their online shopping on the weekends their days off. Make sure

that your auctions don't end until the end of the weekend so they have time to catch the attention of enough people.

9. Offer free shipping when you can. No, you don't have to eat the shipping charges in order to sell. But if you absorb some of the shipping charges in the price, it will benefit you. How? Because items which advertise free shipping automatically get moved to the front of the listings which means much more exposure. This is especially helpful for categories of items with a lot of competition.

10. Offer easy payment options. PayPal is the most common way that buyers are familiar with using. Only accepting cash or credit cards severely limits you. NEVER take checks. You may have to wait weeks for a check to arrive and clear, and you are setting yourself up as a target for scammers. Stick to PayPal.

11. Be efficient. When someone asks a question, answer it. When something sells, ship it in a timely manner with good packing. Keeping your feedback score at or near 100-percent will show potential buyers that you care.

# CHAPTER 8

# Etsy – Making Money with What You Make

If you enjoy arts and crafts, you should know about Etsy.com. Etsy is a website where people can sell handmade goods to those who love and appreciate artistic crafts.

In 2015, Etsy had sales of more than $2.4 billion dollars. As of March, 2016, there were 1.6 million people selling their products on Etsy, and 24 million active buyers, making it one of the most active artist communities on the internet.

The people selling on Etsy are real artists and craftspeople, not commercial mass producers. The buyers on Etsy are people who love buying limited edition and one-of-a-kind artistic pieces. Etsy brings them together where they can meet and benefit.

---

## Getting Started

Are you already creating products? Perhaps you make handmade gifts for friends and family members, or maybe you have even had some experience selling your handcrafts at craft shows or other venues. Ideally you should have a whole line of products that go well with one another.

Choose products that you enjoy making. If you have a big success, you may be making a lot of them!

Make your products unique. If you are selling something customers can buy six other places, why should they buy from you?

Also think about pricing. Can you set a price that is competitive but allows you to be fairly compensated for the time and skill you put in to each item, as well as covering the cost of your materials?

Setting up a store on Etsy is easy. Just go to http://etsy.com and follow the instructions.

## Tips to Attract Buyers

There are three important parts of each listing: The title, the photo and the description.

The title needs to be descriptive in order to get people to click on your item. Use a title that gives useful information, rather than just a name. "Amelia Earrings" doesn't say as much as "Sterling Silver Crystal Drop Earrings." Think about what people might search for when they are looking for what you make, and be sure to include those terms in your title and description.

Great photos are a must! Photos not only need to be clear and well-lit, they should include an artistic element. Look at other photos to get ideas for backgrounds, lighting and other ways to feature your works in the most attractive way possible.

Give a lot of detail in the description. Describe the item, how it was made, its size, weight and any other characteristics. Is there an interesting story behind your choice of materials? Share it!

Lots of people are making money on Etsy. Why not you? Just create a great product, take good pictures and write interesting descriptions. In fact, all you need to do to start making money on Etsy can be done in a day or two.

IF YOU HAVE TO SUPPORT YOURSELF, YOU HAD BLOODY WELL BETTER FIND SOME WAY THAT IS GOING TO BE INTERESTING.
-KATHERINE HEPBURN

# CHAPTER 9

# Your Own Website

Setting up a website of your own is easier than ever. You don't have to be a technical genius to have a great looking website, and it doesn't take a huge budget. Really.

To have a website, you need a domain name and a hosting account.

The domain name is your web address, for example, http://www.idealady.com/. There are lots of places where you can register your domain name. If you are not already using a domain registrar, you can use the service I use: http://GreatDomainsHQ.com/. If you register a domain there, I make a small percentage of your purchase. However, you will find that the prices there are some of the lowest around.

Hosting is where your website "lives" on the Internet. You do not put your website on your personal computer it has to be someplace where it can be accessed by the world 24 hours a day. That is why you need a hosting account. You can find an excellent hosting service that I use and recommend at http://MyFavoriteWebHost.com/. That URL is an affiliate link that will take you to the company I currently recommend for hosting.

So how much does all of this cost? Domain name registration costs $12 or so a year and up. Hosting starts at about $5 a month. There are hosting packages that allow you to host many sites on one account for just a few dollars more each month.

I recommend that you use WordPress (in your own hosting account, not a free site at WordPress.com) to create your site. There are lots of reasons to use WordPress, among them that it is easy to use, millions of others use it so there is lots of support, and the software is free. You can view videos that take you step-by-step through setting up and formatting WordPress on my YouTube channel at http://IdeaLady.tv/.

What about using a free site? Never use a free site for your business. If you don't control your site, you can be put out of business in an instant. Lots of people have started sites on Blogger or WordPress.com.

They posted content, built up the site and sent traffic to it, then one day they woke up and the site was gone. It can happen. They can shut your site down because you violated the terms of service (even inadvertently) or because of complaints or just because.

Some people run their business entirely on Facebook. Right now, Facebook is king of the hill. So was MySpace at one point in time. Remember MySpace? Yeah, I didn't think so. There is nothing wrong with using Facebook and other social media to promote your business, or selling products on Amazon, etsy and other sites. The more places you are, the easier it is for customers to find you. However, you do not want your entire business to be build on someone else's platform. Have a website of your own, with your own domain name on your own hosting account.

Another important part of running an online business is to have an email list. I know people who were getting tons of traffic from Google, really rocking the search engines, and making tens of thousands of dollars a month. Until one day, when Google tweaked their algorithm, and suddenly the traffic went away. The thing that saved their businesses was that they had email lists. When they had traffic coming to their sites, they got some of those people to sign up for their emails. When the traffic went away, they still had a list of people who wanted to hear from them.

Your email list allows you to communicate with customers and prospects. You need an email list. The service I use is Aweber. My affiliate link for Aweber is http://MailYourCustomers.com/. That means I make a small commission when you use my link, but it doesn't affect what you pay. Although I am a big fan of Aweber, you may also want to look at Mail-Chimp and Constant Contact.

If you want to sell from your site, you will need a way to take payments. PayPal is easy to use, millions of people are familiar with it and trust it, and there is no charge to get started. The only cost is that when you receive payments via PayPal, they will retain a few percent (currently 2.9% plus $.30 per transaction) as their fee. There are PayPal accounts that charge a monthly fee, but you probably do not need any of those types of accounts if you are just accepting PayPal at your website. To learn more and get your own PayPal account, go to http://PayPal.com/.

There are other payment processors you can use. On the high end, you can get a merchant account. This is the traditional way businesses accept credit cards and it comes with a boatload of fees. The fees for each transaction can be high, there are monthly fees and monthly minimums and much more. I do not recommend you even consider it unless you are making a high volume of sales every month.

A merchant account lookalike is http://Stripe.com/. It requires a bit more technical skill than PayPal to get it set up, but it can be a good choice if you want something other than PayPal.

There are, of course, many things you can do with a website, but the information in this section can get you up and running with a website of your own.

THE SECRET OF MY SUCCESS IS
THAT I MAKE OTHER PEOPLE MONEY.
AND, NEVER EVER, EVER,
EVER
BE ASHAMED ABOUT
TRYING TO EARN
AS MUCH AS POSSIBLE
FOR YOURSELF,
IF THE PERSON YOU'RE WORKING
WITH IS ALSO MAKING MONEY.
–SIMON COWELL

# CHAPTER 10

# Affiliate Programs

You can add affiliate links to your site to promote products and services offered by others, and make money on the leads or sales you generate for the merchant. Or, you can get other people to sell your products in exchange for a commission by offering an affiliate program. Let's start by talking about how affiliate marketing works.

## What Is Affiliate Marketing?

When you find a program with products or services you want to recommend, you can apply to be an affiliate. Some merchants will approve you automatically, and others will manually review your application before deciding to accept you.

Once accepted, you will be given an affiliate ID and code to place in links to the merchant. For example, your affiliate link might be something like http://www.merchant.com/?aff=456372. You would place this link on your web site or in your email newsletter to refer customers.

Many affiliate programs provide graphics, banners and other advertising materials you can use to promote their products. Some will give you articles and other content to use on your web site or in your email newsletter. Your affiliate link would be embedded in the ad.

When someone clicks on the link, they are taken to the merchant's web site. This might be the merchant's home page or, better, a product or sign-up page. When the person you referred performs a specified action, you earn money. The action might be making a purchase, signing up for a membership, filling out a survey or form, asking for a price estimate or whatever action the merchant is seeking. In some cases, the only action required is a click through to the merchant's site, but that is not typical.

The amount of the payment will vary, depending on the value of the customer. When a purchase is required, you might receive a percentage of the sale amount or a set dollar figure. For lead generation, you would receive a set dollar amount.

In cases where the customer represents long-term value to the merchant, such as memberships, the payment for a new customer can be significant. I have seen payments ranging from under $1 per lead to $35 and up for certain types of leads. When the payment is a percentage of a purchase, it may amount to hundreds of dollars per sale. The most I have received from a single affiliate sale is about $1000, but there are situations where you could earn more.

Most merchants give you a way to log in to your account so you can see how many clickthroughs you have generated, and how much you have earned. Many allow you to include codes in your links so that you can track results by promotion or site. For example, if you promote a product or program on two web sites and in an email newsletter, you would want to know how many customers you got from each source.

Commissions are often paid monthly, but that can vary by program and affiliate. If your earnings are low, they may not be paid out until you have reached a minimum, such as $25 or $50. On the other hand, if you are a "super affiliate" making tens of thousands of dollars, the merchant may be willing to pay you more frequently to keep you happy.

Some affiliate programs have *two tiers*. This means that if someone you refer becomes an affiliate, you would receive a percentage of what that affiliate sells. For example, say that the first tier commission is 25% and the second tier is 5%. You refer customers who buy a total of $1000 worth of products. You would get $250 (25% of $1000) for those referrals. One of your referrals also signs up to be an affiliate for the merchant. He refers additional customers who buy $2000 worth of products. The affiliate you referred would receive $500 (25% of $2000) for his sales, and you would get $100 (5% of $2000) for the sales he referred.

## Getting Started as an Affiliate

Your first step is to find affiliate programs representing products and services you wish to recommend to your customers. There are several ways to do this:

You can look on the web sites of companies you like to see if they have a link that says affiliates, associates, make money with us, or some similar language indicating they have an affiliate program. Click on that link and follow the instructions to sign up.

You can sign up for one or more affiliate networks. Although some merchants run their affiliate programs in-house, many others belong to an affiliate network. These networks may consist of hundreds or thousands of merchants, each with an affiliate program. If you do much affiliate marketing at all, you will probably end up working with these networks.

Some of the leading networks are:

- Commission Junction
  http://www.cj.com/
- Rakuten (formerly LinkShare)
  http://marketing.rakuten.com/affiliate-marketing/
- ShareASale
  http://www.shareasale.com/

You can do a search for one of your target keywords and "affiliate program." Or do a search for "(merchant name) affiliate program." For example, searching for "music" and "affiliate program" brings up several good results, including a link to the iTunes affiliate program (which is managed by LinkShare).

Although some merchants and networks will automatically approve you, others will want to look at your web site before they let you in. You will need to have your website up before you start applying to affiliate programs.

## Once You Are Approved

Each program operates according to its own rules, so when you find a merchant you like, get familiar with what you may and may not do. Merchants may specify where and how you may promote their products, and you may not be able to use any promotional tools other than those supplied by the merchant. Be aware of any rules and follow them. If you don't, you probably won't get paid.

Most programs have a variety of "creatives" you may use. These may include banners, text ads, email ads and more. Using these ads makes it fast and easy to get started with affiliate marketing.

Amazon.com offers something called aStore, that allows you to quickly set up pages of recommended products. You can learn how to set up your own aStore at https://astore.amazon.com/. As an aside, Amazon's Associates program is not the most generous affiliate program out there. However, it is easy to use and they have lots of products available. You can sign up at http://associates.amazon.com/.

## Where to Promote Your Affiliate Links

You can put affiliate links on your web site or blog, or in your email newsletter. On your web site or blog, you can have a section of links or recommended resources where you include affiliate links. For example, I created a page of my favorite resources at http://www.IdeaLady.com/resources where some of the recommendations are through affiliate links.

You could even set up an entire site based on your recommendations. Some people do this by setting up sites called www.(Name)Recommends.com or something similar.

If a site is nothing more than a bunch of affiliate links, though, it will not rank highly in the search engines and will not generate a lot of excitement with users. You may wish to include some good content with your recommendations by writing an article or blog post telling why you recommend this particular product or vendor. Reviews and stories build credibility and interest. Or make a short video where you talk about or demonstrate the product. Do you recommend several similar products? Compare them and let readers know how to make the best choice for their situation.

Create tutorials that show how to do something, and include your affiliate links in the tutorials. Or write an ebook that includes affiliate links. Of course, it should not simply be a collection of links. For example, you could write an ebook about what small businesses need to know about income taxes. There might be a section about using software for accounting and tax return preparation, with links to buy the software. You might have a section on record keeping with links to buy file folders, notebooks to record expenses, etc. A section on hiring a tax preparer could link to tax services. Integrate the links with the text, or have a resources list at the end of each section.

## What to Disclose

Should you let people know that the link you want them to click on is an affiliate link? Most people using the internet today are hip to affiliate links. They know that many merchants offer commissions for referrals. However, the law requires you to disclose affiliate relationships.

On my Resources page, I say right at the top of the page that some of the links are affiliate links, and I may receive a commission if you choose to buy through that link. However, I do not make recommendations for any product unless I truly believe that it is a good product and I have used it or would use it myself. (I say "would use it" because I occasionally recommend something for which I do not have a need; however, I recognize that my clients or audience might. If there is a product I would use if I had the need, I am willing to recommend it.)

I have seen places where in addition to offering an affiliate link, the affiliate will also offer a "plain" link. They usually say something such as, "If you click on this link and buy, I will make a little bit of money. Or, you may click on this other link instead." They may mention that buying through the affiliate link helps to support the site the person is reading. Subtle blackmail? Not really. A lot of people want to give an affiliate commission to a person or site they like. After all, it is a way of supporting them without costing the customer any money as the merchant pays the commission.

Some people choose not to participate in affiliate programs because they do not want to accept money for any recommendations they make. They believe that it taints all of their recommendations if it is known that they are paid for some of them. I certainly respect that position, but I am of the opinion that if I am going to make honest product recommendations, and some merchants are willing to pay me for the referrals, I will not leave the money on the table.

Some of the links in this book and the resources page at IdeaLady.com are affiliate links. As always, whether or not there is an affiliate link attached to a recommendation, the recommendation will only be there if I believe in the product.

# CHAPTER 11

# Avoiding Work-from-Home Scams

A client contacted me one day to ask about an opportunity that had been presented to her. Someone was offering to set her up in an online business that would make money for her without any effort on her part. She didn't really understand how it worked, but it sounded like a great deal. Fortunately, a warning bell went off and it caused her to ask what I thought.

What did I think? If you don't understand it, do not buy into it. If someone cannot explain exactly what the opportunity is, in a way that you can understand, it is not something you should be doing. And if it sounds too good to be true, well, it probably is.

Also ask yourself why they need you. If this business can be set up with little effort and "runs itself," why don't they just keep all the business for themselves?

Don't get so caught up in the idea of making easy money that you suspend your critical thinking abilities. And trust your instincts. My client did, and she turned down the "opportunity."

It is tempting to think that it is possible to make money with no effort, but don't get taken in by the questionable business opportunities promoted by some unscrupulous companies. You've seen the ads:

> Make $1,000 a week stuffing envelopes!
> $5,000 for mailing two letters!
> $100,000 for your signature!

There are many more, but you get the point. Remember what your mother told you? If it sounds too good to be true, it probably is. There are reputable businesses advertising in magazines, but there are some which are less than respectable. Here are a few things to watch for:

Don't send money if you don't know what the opportunity is. Some ads promise lots of money if you follow their "secret" plan, but they don't give a clue what that plan might be.

"Rags to riches" ads are typical of the blind ads described above. The author tells his tragic tale of woe lost his job, kids were sick, wife left, evicted from home, car repossessed, etc. But just when things were at their worst, a millionaire friend gave him the secret to extraordinary wealth. Within days he had thousands of dollars, and now he lives in a mansion with his new blonde wife, a pool and a dozen sports cars. He is going to share his secret with you, for a small fee, of course. Right.

If it sounds too easy, ask yourself why they need you. Some offers suggest that all you have to do is write or visit a company they hook you up with or post an online ad, and you will be given money. If it is that easy, why are they telling you about it?

Watch for the obvious. I have seen ads promising to teach you the secret that will get thousands of people to pay you $5 each. Want the secret? Just send $5! Gee, I wonder what the secret could be?

Don't be fooled by phony "guarantees." They may say something like, "Use this system, exactly as described in our proven plan, for six months. If you haven't made at least $50,000, return it to us. We'll refund your money plus $100." Read it carefully, and you'll see why that guarantee is worthless (aside from the possibility that they will be nowhere to be found in six months).

Don't fall for phony schemes where the only one who makes money is the person who sold you the "surefire" system. And avoid Shiny Object Syndrome, where you keep buying the next new thing that promises instant riches.

Use caution and common sense when evaluating a business opportunity. Many of these scams are successful because people let their greed get the best of them. You don't get something for nothing, you don't get rich overnight (unless you win the lottery) and you don't make money without any effort.

# CHAPTER 12

# Earning What You Need and More

When determining how much you have to earn, it's easy to fall into the trap of assuming that if you are currently making $50,000 a year at your job, you need to earn $50,000 a year as a Solo-preneur. This assumption is wrong on three counts:

- It is based on what you earn, rather than what you spend.
- It does not consider how your expenses may change as a Solo-preneur.
- It does not take into account the tax consequences (both positive and negative) of being a Solo-preneur.

The Monthly Expenses Worksheet in the workbook can help you to calculate how much you will have to earn as a Solo-preneur to maintain the lifestyle you require. That amount may be more or less than your current salary, depending on the changes you expect to make in your lifestyle when you escape the corporate world.

This is a good time to contemplate how you want your life to change, as well as your work. Do you feel that you're in a rat race, and the rats are winning? Think about how you can simplify your life and make it better. Sometimes we get so wrapped up in doing things we believe are expected to us, that we forget to ask ourselves if what we are doing really matters to us or to anyone else. Sort out your priorities, really focus on the important things, and forget about the things that don't matter. Doing so will leave you with more time, more money, and less anxiety.

## Making What You Need

Once you've figured out how much you need to make, you will need to decide how you will earn at least that amount.

Don't confuse how much you gross as a Solopreneur with how much you get to keep. A mistake some people make is thinking that the amount they gross as a Solo-preneur is the same as the paycheck they receive from an employer. As an employee, you are used to receiving a net amount. Your employer withholds money for taxes and forwards those payments to the government, so you may not fully realize the impact taxes have on your earnings. Your employer also pays a portion of your Social Security and Medicare taxes on your behalf, so you don't ever see that. As a Solo-preneur, you have to consider the impact of expenses and overhead in order to determine how much you've made, and you are responsible for paying your taxes to the government out of that money.

Let's see how this works in practice: Jackie had a booth at a crafts fair last weekend and took in $1,000. She looks at all that money and calculates that if she works just two weekends every month, she can make $24,000 a year, and that's what she brings home from her "real job." However, that does not take into account her expenses.

Jackie had to rent a booth for $150, the materials to make her crafts cost $250, and her overhead expenses (e.g., business cards, bags, displays, etc.) are another $50. That means that she spent $450 to bring in $1,000, for a profit of $550. Of course, she owes taxes on that $550, too. Still not bad for a weekend, but it's not $1,000. And if she calculates her hourly earnings, she needs to include not just the hours she spent in her booth at the crafts fair, but also the time she spent traveling to the fair, setting up, and making her crafts.

You can make a good living as a Solo-preneur, maybe even get rich. But be reasonable about your financial needs and how you will meet them. It won't do you any good to make unrealistic projections and then find yourself without enough money to pay your expenses. The goal of Solo-preneurs is to have freedom to live life to its greatest potential, and to experience the joy of doing what you love. If you are always worried about how to pay the rent, you won't be experiencing joy.

## How Much Do You Want to Make?

How much you have to make may be very different from how much you want to make. Perhaps you can meet all of your expenses and have a little left over to save if you make a profit of $30,000. But if you made a profit of $40,000 you would have the money for a down payment on a new car, and if you made a profit of $50,000 you could buy the new car and take that trip to Europe you've always wanted.

Don't be afraid to dream and to strive. If you set your goal at $30,000, you will probably make $30,000 and not any more. We all have a tendency to do as much as is required, or as much as we think we can do. In other words, don't let knowing that you only have to make $30,000 stop you from making $40,000, $50,000, $100,000 or more. Dream big, and you may be amazed at what you can accomplish.

Some call this *visualization*. Lots of people believe that if you visualize something happening, you can make it happen. Many athletes use visualization to supplement their training and practice. An ice skater might imagine herself skating flawlessly through her routine, landing gracefully after a perfect triple-axle, and winning the gold medal. Of course, she still has to practice, but studies have shown that athletes who also use visualization can achieve greater successes.

If you are afraid to speak in public, but feel that you need to do so to become a successful Solo-preneur, imagine yourself giving a speech to a group of people. See yourself in front of the group feeling poised and confident. Hear yourself giving the speech and basking in the applause. Just as the athlete needs to practice, you will have to prepare for your speech. But the visualization can make you more confident in your delivery and lead to overcoming your fears and speaking successfully.

Another method I've found to motivate myself is my dream board. Some people call this a vision board. I bought a piece of poster board and filled it with my aspirations. Your dream board might include pictures of the car you want, the places you plan to visit, your dream house, the cover of the catalog from the college where you plan to send your child, the charitable works you want to support or anything else you dream of. Include quotes that inspire you and the steps you will take to reach your goals. For example, if you know that you have to schedule an average of one appointment a day to get two new clients each month, write a slogan such as, "One a Day = SUCCESS!" on your board.

With confidence and persistence you can achieve all of your goals.

## Establishing Multiple Sources of Income

Once you have determined how much money you have to make, and how much you want to make, the next step is to figure out how you will meet your goals. If your goal is to make $30,000, you may think that there is nothing you can do (other than whatever your job has been) that would generate $30,000. That's probably not true, but if it makes it easier, instead of looking for one thing you can do to earn $30,000, why not look for three ways to make $10,000? These enterprises may be related or not, you may do all of them part-time throughout the year, or you may do each one for only a short time each year.

Once you start Solo-preneuring, the problem will not be coming up with ideas to generate income, it will be finding the time to put them all into action! The great thing about having lots of ideas is that even if some of them don't work out (and some won't) there are always more ideas to take their place.

Have you ever noticed that you always seem to have things come into your life at just the time you are ready for them? The day after you decide you want to take piano lessons, you meet someone who teaches piano. There is a great sale on furniture the week you decide to buy a new couch. You may have met your spouse only weeks or months after you came to the realization that you were ready to marry.

These events are not coincidences. They would have happened whether or not you were ready for them. On meeting the piano teacher you may have said something like, "You teach piano? How interesting," and then forgotten all about the encounter. However, because you were looking, you noticed and took action. You may have money-making ideas everyday, but you have to be open to them before you see them and how they can work for you.

In every other area of your life it seems that people will advise you not to "put all of your eggs in one basket." No financial adviser would recommend putting all of your savings in only one investment. But when it comes to the key to providing financial security for you and your family, everyone from friends to a guidance counselor to your mom will tell you to go find a good job and stay with it. If that's not putting all your eggs in one basket, then what is? We've all learned that the days of getting a job right out of school, staying there for 40 years, then collecting a gold watch at retirement are over. The workforce is changing rapidly. And many people have found themselves pushed out of a company just when they need the job most.

The answer does not lie in the advice commonly given to entrepreneurs, either. The entrepreneur is told to take all his time and money and put it into one concern. Think of nothing else, work on nothing else, and focus completely on making that one venture a success. The reality is that, even with that dedication, a large percentage of entrepreneurial companies do not succeed. So the entrepreneur is left with nothing after working night and day.

And whether you are an employee, an entrepreneur or a Solo-preneur, you will find that seasonal and business cycles impact you. Various types of businesses are impacted differently by these business cycles. If you operate more than one venture, each will react differently to change. One may slow down while another picks up. In this way you are not going to lose all of your income because of changes in the economy.

Don't tie your success to one job, one customer, or even one line of work. Be flexible and follow your wishes and dreams. Start one venture, get it rolling, then start another. The time and energy to manage multiple ventures will be there for you, because the work itself will energize you.

Do you remember The Ed Sullivan Show? Ed often had performers who balanced spinning plates atop high sticks. These performers could keep ten or more plates spinning at a time by following a couple of simple principles: Start them one and a time, and tend each one as necessary. Think of Solopreneuring that way. Start small, then build on your successes. Keep the whole thing in motion by tending whatever requires your attention today. But don't neglect any "plate" for very long, or it may come crashing to the ground!

# CHAPTER 13

# Making Money When You Are Not Working

Employees are used to getting paid for time they don't work. Two weeks of vacation, ten paid holidays, sick days, etc. are available to keep your paycheck coming even when you aren't at work. As a Solo-preneur, you only get paid when you work. There are, however, some things you can do to keep money coming in all the time, whether or not you are working.

**Network Marketing:** Also known as multilevel marketing. Here's how it works: You affiliate with a company by signing up with another dealer. That dealer is part of your "upline," meaning that she makes a commission on your sales as well as her own. As a dealer, you also sell the company's products and sign up other dealers. You make a commission on your own sales, and those of the dealers you signed up (your "downline"). The more you sell and the more dealers you sign, the higher your commissions. While you usually have to be actively selling to collect commissions on your downline dealers, that doesn't mean you have to personally sell product every week.

**Making a Product:** If you manufacture a non-perishable product, you can build up an inventory to cover demand then take some time off. Let's say you sell 100 handcrafted thing-a-ma-bobs every month. If you double your production one month, you'll have an extra month's worth on hand and can take one month off from making thing-a-ma-bobs without suffering a loss of income.

**Commissions and Overrides:** Sales people have always been faced with the reality that if they don't work and sell, they don't get paid. However, some sales create ongoing commissions and overrides. If you sell a life insurance policy, or an ongoing service, on which you are paid commissions, you collect every time the customer makes payment. You may be in the south of France at the time or working on another venture. Overrides mean that you receive a commission on someone else's sales (usually an agent or sales person you brought to the company, as in network marketing). With a little effort, you can build a nice commission income.

**Royalties:** By creating something that will be sold again and again, you may create royalty income. Book authors, recording stars, and other creative types receive royalties whenever one of their creations is sold. They may continue to receive income for years after the book was written or song was recorded. Elvis Presley has probably made more money since his death than he did while he was alive! Maybe you'll never be Elvis, but you could write a book or seminar, or produce an audio or video of your book or seminar, and make royalties on its sale.

**Licensing:** Could you create a design or invention that someone else would license to manufacture and sell? One woman created little clay animals she sold at craft fairs. Hallmark licensed her designs, and she became a millionaire by letting them manufacture the animals she created. You can also license something you've written to be printed in a book, or used as content on a website.

**Rental Income:** Do you own anything that could be rented? Your house, a vacation home, a spare office or even a room in your house could be rented to bring in additional income.

**Sub-contracting:** As your Solo-preneuring ventures become more successful, you may be faced with having to turn down work because you are too busy or don't want to give up your leisure time. Consider sub-contracting with someone else who would welcome the work. You take a fee for arranging the match, the client gets their work done, your associate gets some extra business and increased income, and everyone is happy.

**Contract help:** A variation on sub-contracting, instead of matching the client up with another solo-preneur, you hire someone to do all or a part of the work for the client on contract. You control the relationship with the client and collect all payment, then pay the contractor for the work he or she performed. Check with the IRS for guidelines on when a contractor becomes an employee.

**Investment Income:** As you make profits from your solo-preneuring ventures, invest them wisely.

Over time you can develop income from dividends and interest that will pay you handsomely.

**Selling Your Business:** At some point you may decide that you no longer want to be in a particular business. If you have created something of value to others, the business can be sold. Solo-preneurs may have a harder time doing this than entrepreneurs, because often the solo-preneur is the business. Even if the business consists of a service you provide, and you are a big part of the business, you may be able to sell assets the business has accumulated such as its name, customer list, or other information.

---

## Internet Income

The Internet provides a number of ways to generate income even when you are not actively at work. Most require some effort to set up. Once set up, they can generate profits on a regular basis, some with little or no maintenance. Here are a few examples:

**Sell Advertising on Your Website:** If your site draws enough visitors (at least several thousand page views a month) you may be able to sell advertising.

There are also services that will place advertising on your site for a percentage of the fee paid.

**Join Affiliate Programs:** Affiliate programs allow you to make money by referring visitors from your website to another, where they make a purchase. One of the best known is Amazon.com's program. Typically, you don't pay a fee to join as an affiliate, and you get a percentage of the purchases made by the buyers you refer.

**Create an Affiliate Program:** If you have products to sell, create your own affiliate program and pay a commission to the website owners who send buyers to you. You will need to track your affiliates and purchasers, but there are software programs and services which will do it for you (for a fee, of course).

**Sell at Others' Websites:** I sell books at Amazon.com. Amazon handles the credit card transactions, shipping, etc., then they pay me for the books that sell. After setting up a page for the book, my only effort is to ship books to Amazon once a month or so, and do some promotion for the book. Amazon takes a significant percentage of the sale price, but I have sold thousands of books that I might not have sold otherwise.

**Create Automated Systems to Sell Your Products:** If you are selling information (such as books, special reports, etc.) you can set up an e-commerce site which will take orders, process the credit card transactions automatically, and download a file with the information to the purchaser. All without any direct involvement from you. This is getting easier to do all the time, but it does require that you have some technical expertise, or that you hire someone to set it up. Another option is to offer your digital products through other sites that charge a percentage of sales, but handle all of the transactions. Of course, you will still have to promote your products if you want them to be successful. While you will need to promote on an ongoing basis, you won't have to do so every day.

These are some of the ways you can generate streams of income that are more than an hour's pay for an hour's work. You can probably find additional ways that are appropriate for your products and services and your markets. Be creative: How can you serve your customers in new ways, and create new streams of income for yourself?

# IF YOU DON'T VALUE YOUR TIME,

## NEITHER WILL OTHERS.

# STOP GIVING AWAY
# YOUR TIME AND TALENTS.

# VALUE WHAT
# YOU KNOW

## & START CHARGING FOR IT.

## -KIM GARST

# CHAPTER 14

# Setting Your Prices

*NOTE: Pricing is more art than science. The calculations here are intended to illustrate some of the factors that may be considered when setting prices, but there is not a single formula that will work for every person in every situation.*

Solo-preneurs who perform a service for which they bill by the hour often struggle to come up with an hourly rate. And most of them set their rates too low. Let's take a look at what you need to consider when deciding how much you will charge.

Some people start with how much they were paid as employees. For example, if you were making $50,000 a year at your job, that is an hourly rate of about $24.

$50,000 / 52 weeks / 40 hours = $24.04 per hour

If you are doing similar work in your new business, you may think that is a good rate to charge. That would be wrong.

Your labor only represents one part of the cost of providing the service to clients. In addition to paying you, your employer had to pay other costs associated with employing you, such as employment taxes and benefits. They also had to pay for a place for you to work and whatever equipment and supplies you needed to do your work. There may also be support personnel who enabled you to do your job. You need to factor in all of these expenses when deciding on an hourly rate.

Pricing can be complicated, but let's look at a simple model. We will assume that you want to net $50,000 a year and work about 40 hours a week. We will assume that your costs for overhead (e.g., equipment and supplies) and benefits (e.g., health insurance, self-employment tax) will be $40,000 annually.

That means that you have to earn at least $90,000 to be able to net $50,000 for yourself. Calculating an hourly rate based on $90,000 a year might look like this:

$90,000 / 52 weeks / 40 hours = $43.27 per hour

But we are not done yet. If you plan on working 40 hours a week, those probably will not all be billable hours. Even in a mature business, 50% or more of your hours may be spent on administrative tasks, marketing and down time. You will probably take time off each year for vacation, holidays, sick time and family leave. So let's assume you could bill an average of 20 hours a week, not 40.

$90,000 / 52 weeks / 20 hours = $86.54 per hour

Oh, and one more thing. You should always include an allowance for profit in your calculations. You might assume that your net (the $24/hour we started out with) is your profit, but it is not. That is the cost of labor. Imagine that it is a few years in the future. Your business has multiplied, and you hire 10 additional people to do the same kind of work you are doing now. You need to charge enough to pay their salaries and other expenses. But you also need to make a profit on what they do, or there is no reason to hire them. You might include a margin (e.g., 15%) as your profit. That is the money that goes to you, as the business owner and risk-taker.

So now your hourly rate is right around $100. Remember that we started at $24, but after adding overhead and other expenses, we ended up with a rate about four times that amount.

The next question is whether or not the market will pay that rate. Do some research to determine what your competitors are charging. Are they charging more than $100? Then maybe you should, too. You do not have to have the cheapest rates to get business, and charging much less than your competitors will cause people to doubt your abilities.

What should you do if your competitors are all charging significantly less than $100 an hour? There are several possibilities and the correct answer will depend on you, your business, the market and your competition. If the market is very price sensitive, you may not be able to charge what you believe you are worth. In that case, look for ways to cut your overhead costs. Or see if there is some part of the work you can outsource to someone who charges less than you do. If some of the work does not require a high level of skill, perhaps you could hire someone who is at a lower pay grade than you to do those tasks. Or perhaps it is your market. Maybe a consumer market will not pay your rates, but a business market will. Can you find a group of people who need what you offer and are willing and able to pay your rates? You have a business!

## Successfully Charge More Than
## Your Competitors

You can charge higher prices than your competitors and have customers happy to pay those higher prices.

There's an old joke about the New York City blackout. Power was out everywhere, and the electric company couldn't figure out what was wrong or how to fix it. Finally, they decided that the only one who could solve the problem was a long-retired worker who knew the system inside and out. He came out to the power plant, looked around, picked up a hammer and tapped one of the generators. Suddenly, lights came on all through the area. Overwhelmed with relief that the problem was solved, they asked how much they owed him. "$20,000," he replied. $20,000??? For tapping with a hammer? "Well," he said, "tapping with the hammer is $10. Knowing where to tap is $19,990."

There are a couple of lessons to be learned from this joke. First of all, the value is higher when the problem still exists than after it has been solved. After all, if told he could restore the power for $20,000, officials would have written him the check immediately, without question. Afterward, the problem wasn't so urgent as it had been solved. Quote your price and get agreement while the customer still feels the urgency (and the pain that you will remove). That's when the value is highest to them. Your agreement can include conditions and guarantees, such as the results you will obtain, and deadlines, if they want assurances about results.

Maintain a little mystery. If they hadn't known that all he did was tap with a hammer, his services would have seemed more valuable. After all, they got the result they valued the power was restored. Focus on the results, not exactly what methodology will be used. Don't let customers look behind the curtain. (Remember the Wizard of Oz?)

If you are the only one who provides a particular product or service, or you have skills or training no one else does, the value of what you offer goes up. Highlight your exclusive set of training, education and experience. Use unique language to describe what you do. You can also create an aura of exclusivity by screening clients, and only accepting those who meet your criteria. This can work if you have a reputation already, but it can also help build your reputation, if you've got the guts to try it!

Consider what your clients are used to paying, and charge at least that much. If your clients are used to paying $100 an hour, and you come in at $50, you probably won't get the job. On the other hand, if you can show that you are worth $150, you may be able to charge more than the going rate.

Another way to get an hourly rate higher than others is to charge by the project, rather than the hour. For example, maybe you charge $150 instead of $100 an hour, but you get the job done in fewer hours. Get the client to look at total cost, rather than hourly rates. Once again, get them focused on results.

This issue comes up all the time in my publishing classes, where I remind students that they are not selling paper. They are selling the information printed on the paper information that will improve the lives of the people who use it. Paper is cheap. Useful information isn't.

Keep in mind that the value of your product or service is related to the benefits your customers receive, and how they value those benefits. Present what you sell as solutions to problems, and you can charge premium prices for your excellent products and services.

## Has Your Resume Outpaced Your Abilities?

At an industry conference, I heard a speaker who has a reputation as someone knowledgeable in his field. He even talked about the high fees he charges for speaking and consulting, such as $15,000 for a speech. But he couldn't get through a sentence without at least one "um" or "uh," he went off in new directions without warning, and generally was hard to follow. Listening to him speak was painful, as I was never sure he would actually make it to the end of a sentence.

I found it hard to believe that he gets the fees he claimed, based on what I heard. He may charge those fees, but I don't believe he gets them. What I mean by that is that I believe he has a fee schedule that says he gets $15,000 per speech, but he actually works for free, a reduced fee or a percentage of product sales. Having a fee schedule that says he is a $15,000 speaker sounds impressive, but if he does not deliver a $15,000 speech he loses credibility instead of gaining it.

This is an example of someone whose resume has outpaced his abilities. That is, his claims are greater than what he can produce.

There is nothing wrong with setting high expectations and promising great things. However, if you don't deliver on those promises, you can do serious harm to your reputation and your future. This speaker damaged how I think of him with his poor performance, and I suspect I am not the only one who had that reaction.

Don't misrepresent yourself, especially if your performance will not live up to your representations or your claims are easily disproved.

---

## Pricing Your Products

When your primary business is selling products instead of services, you still need to consider the cost of your labor. Whether you are handcrafting the product or having it manufactured, your time is involved in the creation and marketing of your products.

There are lots of formulas about multiplying the cost of materials to come up with a price for a product, but those formulas are not very accurate. There are many variables to consider in pricing, and the price of every product should include an allowance for your labor in producing the product and running the business.

Also consider distribution costs. Will all of your sales be direct to consumers, or will some be whole-sale to retailers and other outlets? The discount provided to retailers will vary by industry, but as a starting point, assume that you will sell to retailers for about half of the final to-consumers price. It could be less if there are other intermediaries. For example, in the book business, a typical discount schedule would be 40% when selling directly to bookstores, 55% when selling to wholesalers and 65% or more when selling to distributors.

When setting prices, make sure you can sell your product at a price customers will pay, while still covering all of your costs and making a profit.

## Apples and Oranges

One way of setting and getting a premium price is by making an apples and oranges comparison. Comparing your product to a more expensive alternative creates a greater perceived value and makes your product look like a bargain.

You may have seen this done: "My usual consulting fee is $1000 an hour. I charge $3000 for a one-day workshop. But you can get six hours of my expertise, that others have paid $3000 to $6000 for, on these CDs at the low price of just $997."

An apples and oranges comparison should compare similar but different experiences. Comparing the cost of your CD program on buying and selling real estate to the cost of a round-the-world cruise does not make sense. But comparing it to the cost of attending the in-person seminar you recorded does. You might also refer to the fact that they will save time and travel expenses.

## Your Guarantee and Return Policy

People will feel more comfortable buying from you if they know they can get their money back if the purchase isn't right for them. Will some people abuse the guarantee? Sure. But not many. Chances are having a guarantee will help you make more sales, so even if you have a few bogus returns you still come out ahead.

What do I mean by bogus returns? There will be somebody, sometime who buys your item, uses or copies it, then returns it for a refund. Most people are honest, but not everyone. I remember one information marketer telling me about selling a manual that was in a three-ring binder. The buyer returned it saying the information would not work for him. All of the pages were in reverse order, making it clear the buyer had photocopied the manual before returning it. So what did he do? He gave the guy his money back, then flagged him as someone he would never sell to again.

You probably will want to set a deadline for returns. You might be inclined to believe that having a short window during which a refund can be obtained is best. But you would be wrong.

Giving someone a short time may rush them into a decision to return the product. If they have a longer time to evaluate the product, they will take their time. In fact, some may get into the product and end up forgetting about the possibility of a refund.

Depending on the product, you might want to offer a 30-, 60- or 90-day guarantee. You might even consider offering a guarantee of up to one year. Some offer longer guarantees, even "forever."

Do not impose ridiculous conditions on refund requests, although you might ask that the product be returned undamaged.

Do not insist that customers justify a refund request, but it is certainly reasonable to ask why they wish to make the return. If you see several returns come in because customers say the product did not meet their expectations, consider that there may be a problem with the product itself, or your marketing may not properly describe the product, causing customers to have the wrong impression of it.

---

## The Right Price for Your Services

Having the lowest price is not necessarily the way to get more business.

One of the ways people get to know you is by the identity you project. Your company name, the way you present yourself, your web site, your business card and brochure, where you work, and other ways you conduct your business create an image that gives your customers information about you.

Pricing is a part of your image, too. Many entrepreneurs make the mistake of underpricing. They believe that the only way to attract customers is to have the lowest possible price. But this attitude can damage your business.

First of all, when you underprice you won't be adequately compensated for your time. You must be able to make enough money to pay your bills and grow your business, or you won't be in business very long.

Ironically, underpricing can actually result in getting fewer customers, not more. Think about this from the customer's perspective. Let's say you are looking for someone to do a job for you. You contact five companies, and get prices of $4000, $2700, $2500, $2400, and $1000. Which one would you select?

Assuming that the quotes are all based on the same specifications, most people would immediately eliminate the $4000 quote as being way out of line; however, they would also be suspicious of the $1000 quote. Why is it so much less than the others? Do they use substandard materials? Are their workers less skilled? Will they do a poor job if they do the job at all?

Price isn't the only factor people consider when making a purchase. You might choose the $2700 quote because you decide the price is reasonable, and someone from the company called you back quickly. You get a good feeling from their responsiveness, and decide they may be worth a few dollars more than the lowest bidder.

Some markets are more price sensitive than others, and there is probably a price point you can't exceed for your product or service. But coming in far below the "going rate" can be just as harmful to your business as charging too much.

Remember that your prices tell customers how you value your product or service. If you don't value them highly, who will?

And the following is another perspective on pricing that I believe is very important.

## Two Things You Should Never Tell Clients

Potential clients will ask a lot of questions before they hire you. They will want to know about your experience and qualifications, when they can expect the project to be completed and, of course, the price. But there are two pieces of information you should never reveal, no matter how many times they ask, or how many ways they ask.

The first thing you should not let them know is your hourly rate. If you are quoting a price based on a project, then tell them the bottom-line cost. Do not break out pricing based on an amount per hour. We have just spent some time calculating what you should charge per hour, so why would you not tell clients your rate? Because that can get them focused on the wrong thing. If they are employees, they may wonder why you think you are worth $100 an hour when they earn (as you did at your job) $24 an hour. They may not understand everything that goes into that rate.

The second thing you should not talk about is related to the first: how much time it will take you to do some or all of the project. The client has every right to know when they can expect the work to be completed; however, they do not need to know how much time you will spend on the project. For example, you may tell them that you will have the finished project to them in four weeks. But they do not need to know that you will spend a total of 35 hours on the project.

The reality is that as a freelancer you may be working on several projects at once. That may mean spending two days this week on one project, one day on another, and parts of the remaining days on multiple projects. That may be because when you reach a certain point in each project you have to wait for something (e.g., client approval, a proof, a quotation from another vendor, etc.) before you can continue, or it may be because you are juggling several projects and trying to keep everyone happy.

So what should you say when the client asks one of these questions? Get them to focus on the results. If you tell them that the thing you are charging $200 for takes you 15 minutes to do, they will think you are overcharging.

They will not consider, and it may be too difficult to make them understand, that it takes you 15 minutes because you have invested in tools and equipment that give you better results in less time, and that your years of training and experience enable you to do a job in 15 minutes that might take another professional hours. They are likely to fixate on the idea that you are charging them $800 an hour, and nothing you say will convince them that you are worth it. On the other hand, if all they know is that this amazing result cost them just $200, they will be satisfied customers.

Keep the customer focused on the value you provide, not how long it takes you or what your hourly rate is. Then provide value that will keep them coming back for more.

## Should You Ever Work for Free?

There is always a question of when you should give away your expertise, and how much to give away. Some people are opposed to ever giving away anything. However, giving away some of what you know is like giving out samples. When you give people a taste of your expertise, they will want more.

So how much is enough? Start with the expectation that you will give away some content for free. That might mean offering a free email newsletter and posting your articles online, giving free speeches, providing complimentary consultations, distributing free ebooks, offering free teleseminars, etc. Do not assume you have to do all of these things, but look for the ones that are the best fit for your material and your market. If you sell physical products, you may give out samples or offer free trials.

As you begin to establish yourself as an expert, you may find yourself giving away lots. After all, you are building a reputation, and free stuff can make more people aware of you. That is why it is critical that even the products and services you give away for free are of the highest quality. Garbage content will not represent you well.

When should you stop giving away content? Probably never. However, you may find that you shift your unpaid activities from more time consuming to less time consuming. For example, many years ago I gave a lot of free speeches to local organizations. Now, I almost never do. They take too much time that I could use on other, more productive and profitable activities. Instead, I use that time doing paid work or on promotional activities that do not involve putting on makeup and driving across town.

So, how much should you give away for free, and when should you charge?

The justification for giving away free information and services is that by demonstrating your expertise, clients will see how you can help them and will then be willing to pay you. However, you need to decide where the line between free and fee falls for you.

Putting free content, such as articles, on your web site will attract customers and help your standing in the search engines. Articles can also be submitted to print publications, such as professional association newsletters and trade journals, building your expert reputation in your industry.

Publishing articles, online or offline, is a low-risk strategy. You write them once, and your articles remain in circulation indefinitely. They will be viewed by hundreds, thousands or even millions or potential customers. You may even be paid for your articles. Do not put all of your articles into circulation, though. Save some for use only on your own website, or for that book you are going to write.

Clients often want to see a demonstration of your capabilities before they hire you. That might mean putting extensive effort into a proposal, or providing them with a sample of your work. Some clients may ask you to describe how you would solve a particular problem they face, or ask for sample copy or design ideas.

How much time do you want to invest in gathering information and preparing custom work in the hope that it will generate business? When deciding how much you will do during the proposal process, consider the value of the client and the likelihood that you will be able to get the contract. If you do not get the contract, can you re-use the content you put in to the proposal? For example, if you outlined a creative solution to a common business problem, you might be able to turn that into a product of some kind, such as a book, ebook or online course.

Phone calls from information-seekers can be a problem when what you have to sell is your time and expertise. When does answering a question or two cross the line and become an unpaid consultation? Some consultants decide that they will answer two questions without charge. Others place a time limit, such as ten minutes, on free telephone calls. For example, you may transition a freebie-seeker into a paying client by saying, "I can spend ten minutes with you, and if you require more assistance I will be glad to schedule a consultation at my regular rates."

You may also use the questions asked by freebie-seekers as inspiration. If you get a lot of people asking about something, maybe your answer should become a product.

As an expert in your industry, you may be asked to speak to professional and community organizations. Some pay, but many do not. When evaluating a speaking opportunity, consider if the audience includes people who may become customers or who may refer customers to you. And remember that even paid speaking is something for which you are only paid once.

On those rare occasions when I still do free speeches, it is usually because: (1) I am doing a favor for someone in the organization; (2) The group includes a highly-targeted segment of my market; or (3) I want to try out some new material. Just as comedians will jump on stage at a comedy club to try out a new routine, I sometimes test a new topic or presentation by giving a free speech.

Of course, in addition to attracting new customers, some free work may even open new profit opportunities for you. For example, free articles and speeches may lead to a profitable new career as an author and speaker. Many experts became professional speakers because after delivering a freebie someone came up and asked, "How much would you charge to speak to my company?"

Even better, record your speeches and they become audio products you can sell, so that you get paid again and again for your "free" speech.

Only you can decide where the line should be between free and fee. No matter what you decide is right for you today, revisit your free activities every few months or so to see if it is time to change the amount of time and effort expended on freebies, or if the nature and type of free things you offer should change.

## When (and How) to Say No to Free

A while back I got an email from someone who wanted to meet with me so he could ask some questions. Think about what he was asking: He wanted me to get in my car and drive somewhere to meet up with him, so I could give him answers for free, of course, that he could have gotten by buying my book. But the book would cost him a few bucks, so that was not a good solution.

I thought I would be nice, so I asked him to email a couple of questions that I would answer for him. He insisted that we had to meet and discuss this in person. Well, I don't even do paid consultations in person anymore, so I told him we could set up a telephone consultation and told him my rates. His response? "Well, if you are going to charge me, forget it!"

That is the kind of "customer" that I am more than happy to see go. In fact, I would gladly have given him the names of a few of my competitors so he could waste their time instead of mine. (No, that would be bad karma. ;o) )

There is nothing wrong with giving away some things for free, whether you are establishing a new business or you have been around for ages.

I give away a lot of free content, sometimes do free teleseminars and webinars, and answer the occasional question. However, it is important to know where to draw the line, and how to say no to people who want more than you are willing to give. For me, there is a firm line when it comes to giving away my time for little or no return.

Here are some tips to help you figure out when and how to say no to free.

**Set limits.** There are always people who will call or offer to take you to lunch to "pick your brain." That is called free consulting, and it is a mistake to do it. If someone calls with questions, and you want to help them, set a limit right up front by saying something such as, "I have 10 minutes right now. If you need more time than that, we can schedule a consultation at my regular rates."

**Leverage the free stuff.** Spending a lot of one-on-one time giving free advice is probably not the best use of your time. When you are going to do something for free, look for the activities that will give you the best results and best reach for the time you invest. Instead of having lunch with one of those people who want to pick your brain, hold a teleseminar and invite everyone on your list. Record the teleseminar and give the recording to everyone who signs up for your email list, or sell it as a download or on CD. Spend that hour reaching thousands of people instead of just one.

**Limit access.** Have someone else deal with your phone calls and emails so you don't get in the position of responding to routine questions that can become time consuming. That also gives you a buffer so that your assistant is the one saying no to unreasonable requests, not you. Set up a help desk and get a virtual assistant to handle inquiries. (Many webhosting companies, including the one I recommend at http://MyFavoriteWebHost.com/, offer free help desk scripts.)

**Establish a pro bono budget.** Just as you set a budget for how many dollars you can donate to worthy causes, set a budget regarding the time you can spend on free work. It is fine to do some unpaid work to help worthy groups or individuals, but you will find yourself overwhelmed with "opportunities" to work for free unless you have a firm policy about how much free work you will do and how you decide for whom you will work pro bono.

**Don't be afraid to ask yourself, "What's in it for me?"** When you are asked to do something without pay, there is nothing wrong with choosing the unpaid work that benefits you in some way over that which does not. If you only have time for one unpaid speaking engagement this month, choosing the one that allows you to speak to a room full of potential customers while turning down another that is unlikely to result in any business for you is the only sensible thing to do.

Only you can decide how much you are willing to do for free. However, don't get caught in the trap of giving away more than you want to because of the unreasonable expectations of others or because you are unwilling or unable to say no.

Establish a firm policy about what you will do without pay, and stick to it.

# MONEY IS A TERRIBLE MASTER · BUT · AN EXCELLENT SERVANT.

➡ ~ P. T. BARNUM ⬅

# CHAPTER 15

# Managing Money

When you go from receiving a paycheck every week to the world of Solo-preneuring, you have to make an adjustment in the way you look at money. Instead of the predictable amount you received every week, money will come in drips and drops at some times, and in torrents at others. It is up to you to manage your money so that the torrents you receive will get you through the drips and drops days.

**Learn about money.** Most of us are woefully ignorant when it comes to money. Understand how money is earned and how it grows, and you will be on your way to financial security.

**Always put money aside.** Have an account you don't touch where you can deposit a portion of your earnings to meet your tax obligations. Have another account where you park extra cash to use during a dry spell.

**Use credit wisely.** Credit can be a trap or a tool, depending on how you use it. If you run up credit card bills buying lots of things you don't need (and may not even want) you are not a wise credit user. But, if you use credit cards to take advantage of the "float," they are a wonderful tool. If you need to buy something to complete a job for which you will be paid. charge the expense today, and pay the bill when it arrives, out of your revenue.

**Keep a trick or two up your sleeve.** It is a good idea to always have one or two ways you can generate quick cash, especially during start up. It could be anything from setting up at the farmer's market to sell your herbs to temping in an office for a few days. Once your business is established, you may be able to generate extra income by calling on past customers and offering additional products or services. Just knowing where the money will come from will give you peace of mind, and you won't waste a lot of time trying to figure out what to do when the day comes that you need the extra money.

The most important adjustment you may have to make, though, is in your mind. Abandon the idea that a paycheck equals financial security (it doesn't) and make your own security.

---

## Full-Time, Part-Time or Spare Time

You decide how often and how many hours you wish to work as a Solo-preneur, so you may work 40 or more hours each week, you may take every third week off, you may work 60 hours a week for six months then not at all for six months, or however you choose.

If you are currently employed, you must decide if you are going to take the leap into Solo-preneurship, or slowly wade in by starting in your spare time. You may be wondering, "Who has any spare time?" but what I've observed is that we make time for those things that are important, and we make excuses for the rest. If taking charge of your life is important, you will find the time.

As an employee, you have the advantage of a regular paycheck and benefits while you plan and establish your business. That gives you time to build the profits from the business, without the pressures of having to meet all of your expenses out of those profits.

I was able to launch some of my Solo-preneuring ventures while I was still employed, because I saw that I was going to be laid off in the future. If I had it to do over again, I would have started even before I saw that layoff coming. There is so much I could have learned (and extra money I could have made!) if I had taken my first steps sooner.

There are reasons, though, to take the plunge and go into Solo-preneuring full-time. You may not have a choice. If you are laid off or fired, you are suddenly faced with having to make a living somehow. Your business may be able to get in on a trend or business cycle that makes it important that you start right now and devote your full attention to the business.

And, finally, that paycheck can be a security blanket that keeps you from getting out on your own. Make sure the illusion of security you receive from a paycheck does not keep you from striking out on your own and following your dreams. Set deadlines for yourself, and meet them. Give yourself a set period of time to establish your business and make it profitable, determine what you have to do to make that happen, then do it.

# Setting Up Your Business

When you start there are several things you need to do to establish your business. This chapter covers some of the most important decisions you need to make and actions you should take when starting a new business.

## Choosing a Name

Depending on the nature of your business, you may do business under your own name or you may use a company name. Many consultants and other service providers do not use a company name. The advantage of doing so is that there is no paper work to file, and there are no special requirements for opening a bank account. The disadvantage is that your name doesn't tell potential clients what you do.

If you do business under a company name (or "assumed name") you can choose a name that is catchy and expresses what you do. Don't underestimate the marketing benefits of a good name. In addition to helping you market your business, using a name other than your own can make it easier to create a business you can sell. After all, there might be a market for Technology Consulting Associates, but not for Amy Jones.

Filing as a corporation may also provide some protection from your business' creditors in the event of financial problems. (It's not as foolproof as you may think, however. See the following section on Form of Business for more information.)

Your assumed name is possibly the most important part of your business identity. Many people spend very little time naming their business. Don't make this mistake! The name is typically the first thing potential customers know of your business, so it should say a lot about what you do. Be sure to keep these things in mind when selecting a name for your business:

A good business name defines what you do. "Smith-co" doesn't say anything about the business, except that it is probably owned by someone named Smith.

On the other hand, "American Deck and Patio" tells you a lot about that company.

Don't be too narrowly focused. "Johnson's Health Insurance Brokers" may be too specific. If you also decide to offer life, disability, and other types of insurance, it won't be obvious to potential customers. "Johnson's Insurance Brokers" might be a better choice.

Don't limit yourself geographically. "Southwest City Maid Service" may be okay today when you are cleaning houses by yourself. But if you decide to expand and take on contract help, you will want to take on clients in other parts of the city, and your name may put them off or make them think you won't serve them.

Do a national trademark search before settling on a name. You may only plan to do business in your town, but who knows what the future will bring? You don't want to find out that someone else is using the same name in an area where you plan to do business. If they hold a national trademark on the name, you may even be forced to change your business name.

Don't forget your website. When choosing a name, consider what the URL (address) of your website will be, and make sure the one you want is available. If it is, register it immediately as it may be claimed by someone else by tomorrow.

See the section on Licensing and Registrations for more information on filing your company name.

## Form of Business

The three most common forms of legal structure are:

- Sole proprietorship
- Partnership
- Corporation

**Sole Proprietorship** - The easiest form to set up is the sole proprietorship, and this is also the most common form of structure for the small business or Solo-preneur. As a sole proprietor, although you may have employees, you are solely responsible for the business. That means you keep all the profits, and pay all the debts. Because you and the business are one and the same in the eyes of the law, your personal property can be seized by creditors to satisfy business debts. Earnings or losses from the busi-

ness are reported on Schedule C of your personal
income tax return.

Advantages:
- Easy to start
- You make all decisions and have control
- All profits are yours

Disadvantages:
- You have personal liability for business debts
- No provision for continuation at your death
  or retirement

**Partnership** - A partnership may be created when
two or more persons own a business. Solo-preneurs
may find that they wish to partner with someone in
one or more ventures. You may choose a general
partnership where all parties are active in the business, or a limited partnership where one or more
parties are not active in the business, but have con-
tributed financially. A limited partnership must have
at least one general partner actively involved in the
business.

Partnerships may be 50 / 50 or any other split agreed
upon by the partners. Whatever your arrangement,
be sure to put all of the terms and conditions of the

partnership in writing. It's wise to consult an attorney when drawing up a partnership agreement.

As with a sole proprietorship, partners report earnings on personal income tax returns, and the partners are personally liable for business debts.

Advantages:
- Pooling of assets and skills
- Easy to start, with little regulation

Disadvantages:
- Control shared by partners, conflict possible
- Personal liability for debts of the partnership, including debts incurred by others

**Corporation** - The corporation is the most difficult and costly form of business to set up and maintain, but it does provide some advantages. Principal among them is protection of your personal assets from business creditors and legal judgements against the business. When you incorporate, you create another legal entity. The corporation is separate from you; for example, filing its own income tax return rather than reporting its earnings on your return.

However, there is a trend among creditors and litigants to attempt to "pierce the corporate veil" and seize personal assets. This can be successful if the owner of the corporation have not complied with all of the laws and regulations regarding maintaining the corporation.

If you think incorporation would be best for your business, consult an attorney to be certain that all legal requirements are met.

Advantages:
- Limited personal liability
- Separate legal entity with transferable owner-ship

Disadvantages:
- Costly to form and maintain
- Heavily regulated
- May lead to double taxation of income taxed once at the corporate level and once at the personal level

In addition to these three forms, there are many variations which incorporate elements of more than one of the above forms. Check with an attorney or your state's Secretary of State or Department of Commerce for more information. You may also be able to get information from your County Clerk's office, or from a local office of the Small Business

Administration or Small Business Development Center.

## Licensing and Registration

Most cities, counties and states have regulations requiring licensing or registration of businesses. For information about what is required in your area, contact the county clerk's office or your state's department of commerce. You can also get information from your local Small Business Administration office. As an example of what to expect, here are some issues to think about when setting up your business:

If you are doing business under any name but your own (e.g., Smith's Services rather than John Smith) you will need to file an assumed name or DBA ("Doing Business As"). This may be filed with the county or state.

Incorporating is usually handled through the Secretary of State's office in your state of operation. You may incorporate in another state if you wish. Many companies incorporate in Delaware or Nevada, due to favorable laws in those states.

You will need information on collecting and remitting sales tax if you sell taxable goods or services. You'll also want a tax certificate in order to avoid paying sales tax on items you are buying for resale. (If you are buying products and reselling them to your customers, you wouldn't pay sales tax when you buy the products, but your customers would pay sales tax when they buy them from you. You would then be responsible for remitting the sales tax to the state.) Contact the state comptrollers in your states of operation for information about sales tax regulations.

Many types of professions (e.g., doctors, barbers, therapists, etc.) and businesses (e.g., food service) require special licensing. Contact your city or state to learn if licensing is required for your business.

To get a federal tax ID number assigned, go to the Internal Revenue Service website at http://IRS.gov/. If you hire employees, you will need a tax ID number (an EIN) but even if you don't have employees, you may want one. You can give the EIN instead of your Social Security Number when you get paid by clients. That can reduce your risk of identity theft.

You'll also need information about what taxes you are required to withhold from employees' pay, and how often the taxes must be forwarded to the IRS. Planning to use contractors instead of employees? Get the IRS publication that gives the current regulations on when someone is considered a contractor vs. when they are an employee.

The IRS has a number of publications available about small business taxes. You can download them online or get printed copies from the IRS. Also check with your local library, as they may have copies of these publications available. Look for information about quarterly tax payments, too. When you have self-employment income, you may be required to file quarterly returns to avoid penalties. If you are planning to take a deduction for a home office, ask for the current IRS rules.

Your state may also require an employer identification number.

If you have employees, contact your state's Workers' Compensation department for information about regulations which apply.

Also, if you have employees there are zillions of federal laws and regulations to deal with. Don't ignore these laws as your ignorance could be costly in fines, litigation expense, and court judgements. Know the laws and regulations that apply to you and follow them.

The Americans With Disabilities Act (ADA) may also affect you if you have a facility (e.g., a store) that is accessed by the public.

To register a trademark or patent, visit the Patent and Trademark Office on the web at http://www.USPTO.gov.

For information on how to register a copyright on material in written form or other media (e.g., software, film, music, etc.) go to the website of the Copyright Office of the Library of Congress at http://www.Copyright.gov/.

## Getting Paid

Depending on the nature of your business, you may invoice customers, receive cash and checks, or accept credit cards. The more ways customers can pay you, the better it is for both you and them.

It used to be difficult to get a merchant account in order to accept credit cards, especially for small and home-based businesses. The good news is that now there are several companies competing for your business.

You can accept payments at your website with (among others):

- PayPal
- Amazon Payments
- Google Wallet
- Apple Pay

Each of these can work well, although each may have limitations. Also consider using Stripe to accept credit cards.

I have a merchant account that allows me to accept credit cards at my website, and I also accept PayPal. Merchant accounts are expensive. There are monthly fees and minimums, and the percentage you pay for each transaction is impossible to know. If I were starting out today, I would only offer PayPal. Many people buying online have a PayPal account but, even if they don't, they can still pay with a credit card via PayPal.

Offline credit card payments are easy, if you have a smart phone or tablet. There are several services that will give you (or sell you) a reader that plugs in to your device. Use it to swipe customers' credit cards, and a day or so later, the money is in your account. Easy as can be, and the rates they charge are low. No monthly fees or minimums, and reasonable percentage charges. You are not limited to using one.

I have devices from:

- Square
- PayPal Here
- Amazon Register

All three work very well and have similar costs associated with them. There are others out there, and there will be more to come. Just choose one or try as many as you like.

# BUILD YOUR OWN DREAMS,

{ OR SOMEONE }

# ELSE WILL

**HIRE**

YOU TO BUILD

THEIRS.

{ -FARRAH GRAY }

CHAPTER 17

# Start Up Costs

The amount of money you'll need depends on the type of business you've selected, what equipment and materials you must buy, the form of business you've decided on, and whether you are starting out part-time or full-time.

Don't delay following your dream because you think you need more money. While some businesses require a lot of cash, look for a way to take the first step toward your dream business with less money.

When I decided to get into the seminar business, all the information I found said that the startup costs would be $5,000 to $20,000. I wasn't willing to accept that, so I found another way. I started presenting seminars through an organization that promotes seminars in return for a percentage of the fees. My only upfront cost was $10 for a listing in their schedule. I used the profits from my first seminars to start promoting my own seminars (at much less than $5,000) and I presented seminars through that organization for years because it was profitable for me.

Likewise, when I wanted to start my publishing company, I started with an investment of $200. The very first day I started selling my books, I made back my initial investment with a profit (and I hadn't even sold all of the books I printed).

If your dream is to start a store, what steps could you take toward that dream on a small budget? You could sell at flea markets, rent a small space within an existing store, or even sell your goods at home parties. Be creative, and you can think of many alternatives. Use your profits to finance the dream version of your business, and you have several advantages. First of all, you won't have debt (or you'll at least have less debt), you get to learn about business without a lot of expensive mistakes, and you build a customer base which can help make your dream happen and become successful faster.

The people and books telling you that you need thousands of dollars to start a business assume that you are going to start "large." You don't have to start out doing the same things that larger, more established companies do. Start on a smaller scale and build. That's probably what most of those big companies did.

Starting out with more desire than cash can be a challenge, but it keeps you focused on doing what is really important. Having a lot of cash leads to what I call the "Spending is progress" theory. This is when you think that spending money on furniture, equipment and supplies brings you closer to your goal. It may feel productive, but it's not. Getting your product or service out in front of the people who will pay for it is productive, and it will lead to making money.

One of the advantages of Solo-preneuring is that you can keep your start-up costs as low as you need to. Some profit centers will require absolutely no investment, and many others require little more than the cost of printing some business cards. If you wish to pursue a profit center that will require an investment, see if you can fund it with the profits from another of your income sources.

If you do not have another source of income, you need to be certain you have adequate capital to fund your living expenses until you can support yourself on the earnings from your business. Savings or severance pay can be a great help.

## Sources of Funding

Funds to start your business can come from many sources. You may have adequate savings both to pay your start-up expenses and fund your living expenses as well. If you were recently laid off, you may have severance funds to help with your start up.

If you can't (or don't wish to) fully fund your business yourself, you can borrow funds from your bank, credit union, family or friends. Be cautious about borrowing, and especially using credit cards to fund your start up. Credit cards typically charge a fee for each cash advance, and charge a high rate of interest. They should be used only as a last resort.

# CHAPTER 18

# Setting Up Your Office

Keeping costs low is important to most Solo-preneurs, and avoiding the costs of leasing an office will help. Starting a business on your kitchen table is probably not realistic. However, you may not need a huge office dedicated to your business. A corner of the bedroom, or a spot in the basement, or almost anywhere you can find enough space will do.

First, determine what your space needs are. What equipment is required (computer, sewing machine, etc.)? How much space is required for supplies, records and reference books? What about work space for assembling products or mailings? And don't forget storage space so that files and equipment not in use can be put away.

Next, consider what amenities are required. Do you need a phone line or Internet access? Is there adequate lighting? Are there enough electrical outlets?

Where will your space be? If you need to be away from distractions, try to find a place where you won't be disturbed. You need to feel comfortable in your space. If you want to be able to look outside while you work, make sure there is a window with a view.

Consider how you will handle meeting with clients, if that is an issue. You may be able to visit clients in their homes or offices. That can actually be an advantage to your clients, as they get the convenience of you coming to them rather than they coming to you.

Some executive suites will rent offices and meeting rooms for a few hours or a day, so you can hold meetings, seminars and other events there. You may be able to barter for the use of a friend's office. Libraries have meeting rooms which can be reserved. Of course, you can always meet at a restaurant or coffee shop. Consider what is most appropriate for customers in your industry when choosing a meeting place.

Will you find it hard to work at home? Some people find that the distractions of being at home (the television, people dropping in, having the refrigerator close by, etc.) keep them from working effectively.

Or, they may feel more comfortable with other people around. If that's the case for you, take some "road trips" to help you get in the mood to work. I like to go to the library sometimes, just to be away from my home office for a while. Some people like to work at a restaurant or coffee shop. Some office supply stores and print shops have workstations where you can sit and work for a while. (I often use these when I'm out of my office and have time between appointments.)

If you find that you absolutely cannot work at home, here are some tips for finding an affordable office:

Consider an executive suite. Tenants each have one room for an office, but there is a common reception area and typically a shared conference room and kitchen area. The executive suite may provide a receptionist, fax, photocopier and phone system.

There are several shared office spaces where you can drop in and use a desk when you need it. You may pay a monthly fee for access, or only pay when you use it. To find one in your area, do a search for "coworking spaces."

Look for an opportunity to share office space with another professional. You might be able to find a compatible roommate and save money.

Seek out a sub-let. Someone may have an unexpired lease on space which they are not currently occupying, and they may offer below-market rent to recoup some of their costs.

## Your Mailing Address

If you are doing business from your home, you may not want to use your home address as your business mailing address on business cards and other communications. There are options, each with its pros and cons.

Renting a post office box from the USPS is inexpensive, and it is unlikely that they will go out of business. The post office will forward your mail for up to a year if you move and close the box. However, some people still think a P.O. box represents a shady business. And you can not receive packages shipped via FedEx or UPS at a post office box.

Private mail boxes give you a street address, and they will accept packages shipped via any service. The risk is that the company can go out of business and leave you with no way to get your mail. The post office will not forward mail sent to a private mail box address. This can be a disaster if you have checks, orders, invoices and other mail coming to a private mail box that suddenly disappears.

It happened to me. I had a private mail box for 15 years. One day, I came back from an out-of-town trip to discover they were closed. Fortunately, the business owner picked up our mail at the post office every day for a month, and arranged for us to get it from another private mail service just down the street. The new service was even nice enough to give us a credit on our box rental for rent we had already paid to the other business.

Even so, it was a nightmare. I had put that address on websites, business cards and many other places, including printing it in the books I published. Several businesses I dealt with had that location as my mailing address. I think I eventually got them all corrected, but I will never know for sure.

One thing I do now is that I have almost all important mail (e.g., checks) sent to my home address.

Also, I do not publish a street address in my books, just my website URLs. The mailing address is listed at several of my websites, but that is easily corrected if it changes again. And I now use a P.O. box, so my mail can be forwarded if my address changes.

You may not even need a mailing address—how often will people be mailing things to you? I use the P.O. box as my contact information on my domain name registrations, but not for much else.

---

## Setting Up Your Office – Zoning

Many cities and towns are not user-friendly to home based businesses. Even cities without zoning may have deed restrictions or regulations limiting or prohibiting home based businesses. If you live in such a place, you should consider leasing an office.

First, though, find out exactly what activities are prohibited. It may be that any business activity is prohibited, or it may be that only businesses with public traffic (retail stores, beauty salons, etc.) are prohibited. Many times, the work Solo-preneurs do in their home offices may involve just the Solo-preneur sitting at a computer (not an activity likely to catch the attention of the neighbors).

If you are determined to proceed in violation of zoning regulations, it would be a good idea to learn what penalties are applied if you are caught running a home business. In many cases, you are ordered to cease operations at home, but there is no fine or other penalty. You may decide that you're willing to take your chances if that is the case. If you work from home in violation of the regulations, you should have a plan in place to continue your business if you required to move it from your home.

While the objective of most businesses is to attract a lot of attention, it's a good idea to avoid getting the attention of your neighbors when you're working out of your home (even if you're not violating any rules by doing so). If you create any disturbance for the neighbors, you encourage them to turn you in (if there's a rule against home businesses) or get a law passed against home businesses (if there isn't one on the books). Follow a few common-sense rules:

Don't have a lot of traffic coming through the neighborhood to see you. Go to your clients instead of having them come to you.

Limit the number of deliveries you have coming to your home. Have packages delivered to a mail drop, or pick them up yourself.

Don't put your home address on business cards, if possible. If your clients never come to your office, you can use a post office box or mail drop address, or simply leave the address off the card. Or, look in to business identity programs offered by some executive suites.

## Setting Up Your Office - Equipment and Supplies

The equipment you need depends of the types of profit centers you will have. What you are able to purchase at start-up depends on the money you have available. While you may think it desirable to have a bunch of brand new equipment, at least some of that expense could probably be postponed until the equipment can be purchased from the profits you have generated.

Most businesses these days require the use of a computer, but that doesn't mean you need to buy the latest-and-greatest. The computer you already have will probably be just fine.

Beyond that, you will probably need basic office supplies and any supplies or equipment specific to your business.

---

## Setting Up Your Office - Tax Considerations

Tax regulations are always changing, so be sure to refer to IRS publications and other guides for current tax information. The IRS has free seminars for businesses to explain what records are required, how regulations affect business, etc. Attend one in your area if you need clarification or want the opportunity to ask questions.

It may be possible to deduct expenses for the portion of your home you use as office space. If you qualify you can deduct a portion of your rent or mortgage payment, utilities, and other costs of maintaining your home.

The equipment you purchase is generally deductible to the extent it is used for business. That means that if you use your computer 80% for business and 20%

for personal tasks, you may be able to deduct 80% of the cost.

Furniture and supplies are also deductible, if they are used for business purposes. Major purchases, such as computers and furniture, may have to be amortized over a period of three to ten years. That means that you can only deduct a portion of the cost each year until you have deducted the entire amount. Ask your accountant or the IRS if you qualify for a Section 179 deduction where you can deduct some major purchases in one year, instead of amortizing.

# CHAPTER 19

# Recordkeeping and Taxes

It is critical that you keep detailed financial records of your business. Of course, the IRS will be interested in how much you made. If you fail to report income, you will hear from the IRS.

It's also important that you document your expenses so that you can take all of the tax deductions to which you are entitled. The deductions are in the tax code because it is recognized that you had to spend money to make money. Therefore, you are not taxed on the part of your income you had to spend to generate other income. There is nothing wrong with taking every deduction you can document. It is legal and right to do so. But in the event you are audited someday, you must be able to back up every deduction to the satisfaction of the IRS.

Perhaps the most important reason to keep good records is to know how your business is doing. If you don't know how much it costs you to do something or make something, you won't know how to price it and you won't know if you are making a profit. This is especially true when you have several profit centers, and other profit centers may be carrying one very unprofitable center.

If you are not an accountant, it may pay to hire one. Whether you hire an accountant or not, get a book about bookkeeping or take an accounting class so that you understand how money flows through your business.

---

## Federal Taxes

Keep up with changes in the federal tax code by requesting current publications from the IRS. They have several that are designed to help the small businessperson determine their rights and obligations under the tax code. Contact your local IRS office and ask when their next small business tax seminar will be, and make plans to attend, or refer to IRS.gov.

In addition to income taxes, you are required to pay Social Security and Medicare taxes on your profits.

These taxes are remitted with your federal income tax payments.

Self-employed persons are required to pay their federal taxes quarterly. Failure to file quarterly returns can result in expensive penalties and interest on the unpaid taxes.

Make sure you follow all of the regulations, report your income, and file your returns on time. Also take every deduction to which you are entitled, and do not pay any more tax than you are required to pay. Paying more than you owe will not protect you from a random audit, and doesn't earn you a gold star. It just costs you money.

## State and Local Taxes, and Sales Taxes

Depending on where you live, you may also be required to pay state and local income taxes. Check with state and local authorities for information on when and how to file. You may be required to file quarterly, just as for federal taxes.

If you sell products or services which are subject to sales tax, you will have to collect and remit sales tax to your state. Check with the State Comptroller's office, or other taxing authority for more information. Generally you are required to obtain a permit to collect taxes, and file your returns at least quarterly.

With a tax permit, some of your purchases may be tax-exempt. If you are purchasing an item for resale, you do not pay sales tax when you purchase it, but your customers do when they purchase it from you. You are still required to pay sales tax on items purchased for your use. For example, if you purchase printers and resell them to your clients, you don't pay sales tax when you buy the printers, but you collect sales tax from your customers and remit it to the state. If you buy a printer for your own use, you pay sales (or use) tax on the printer.

You may also be exempt from paying taxes on equipment you purchase to use in the manufacturing process. For example, if that printer you bought is used to print books that you sell, or for transfers which you print on t-shirts you sell, you may not have to pay sales tax on the purchase of the printer and related supplies.

# CHAPTER 20

# Getting Customers

Now that you've thought of what you can do to earn a living without a job, the next step is to find people who will pay you for the things you plan to do. Even the best business ideas are worthless without paying customers.

Many people who start new businesses go through all the steps of buying equipment and supplies, registering their business name, printing business cards and stationery, and then sit there waiting for customers to start knocking on the door. It doesn't work that way! You have to get out there and tell people who you are, what you do, and why it matters to them. Don't assume that people will flock to your website, either. They have to know it is there, and they have to have a reason to go there.

When asked why he robbed banks, it's claimed that Willie Sutton said, "Because that's where the money is." To get customers for your business you have to figure out who would want or need what you have to offer, then go where they are.

Marketing may mean selling getting in front of people, telling them about you and your product and asking them to buy. If you're thinking you can't do it, that you've never been good at sales, then make sure you have at least one income source that doesn't require you to find customers. Do contract or temporary work through an agency, sell your crafts at a crafts mall, or work part-time for someone else. Then get used to the idea of selling, and go out and start finding customers for your other ventures.

Start changing your mindset about marketing and sales now. Even if you've never been good at sales, that may be because you were trying to sell something you didn't believe in. When you feel passionate about something, it doesn't feel like selling, it just seems like you are sharing something really wonderful with others.

Can you remember a time when you found a great new product, or a wonderful restaurant? You told everyone you thought would be interested, right? You didn't think of that as selling, you were just telling them about something that you believed would make their lives better in some way. When you are offering a product or service you believe in, that's what you do. When you tell potential customers about it you tell them about something that can make their lives better.

But marketing is more than the actual process of selling. It is the whole process of deciding how you will present yourself and your product to people, which people would want your product, and how to get your message to them.

## How to Get Your First Customer

The first customer can be the hardest one to get, but these ideas will help you land that first customer quickly and easily.

Typical advice given to new businesses is to give away their services or charge steeply discounted rates in order to get experience and build a customer base. This can work, but it is a dangerous strategy. First, because those first customers may not value your work if they are not paying market rates, and second, because the time you spend working for nothing or next-to-nothing might be used more effectively in marketing to customers who will pay full price.

When you have attracted customers by giving them bargain-basement prices, those customers may not stick around when you try to charge market prices. Plus, bargain seekers can be more demanding that customers paying full price, so you may end up spending more time than you expected providing service.

There are times when it makes sense to work for free or almost free. For example, if you are volunteering for a charity you support, or if you are building your portfolio or making contacts, it can be worthwhile. As a major strategy for getting your first clients, though, it is not your best choice.

Here are some other ways you can find the clients you need to get your business off the ground.

**Meet the new boss, same as the old boss.** If you recently left a corporate job, your former employer could be a good prospect for your new business. You understand their business, they know what you can do, and the stage is set for them to become your first customer in your new enterprise.

**Get your net working.** Contact people you know and tell them about your new business. Let them know you are actively seeking new clients and what you can do for those clients. Do you think it is hard to call people and ask for their business? Get over it, but in the meantime, instead of asking for their business, ask if they know someone who could use your services.

**I'll show you mine if you show me yours.** Barter with other businesses for products and services you need through an informal exchange or a barter network. When you barter and get something you truly need in return, it is as good as cash and it is not the same as working for free.

**Try it, you'll like it.** Clients may be reluctant to commit to a high-dollar or long-term contract with an unknown and unproven business. Give them a lower-cost way to try you out that compensates you fairly, such as a small project, or give them an out in the contract if you do not meet performance goals.

**Get visible.** Speak to community and professional organizations. Join the Chamber of Commerce and networking groups. Get active in your professional association. Find ways to get in front of people that can become customers.

**May I borrow a cup of customers?** When you do not have customers of your own, use the ideas in the section of this book about borrowing customers from other businesses.

Choose the strategies that are the best fit for you and your business, and put them to work. You will have your first clients in no time!

---

## Advertising

Not all advertising is created equal. Where you should advertise, and even if you should advertise, depends on the types of products and services you have to offer, and who your target market is for those products and services. For many Solopreneurs, advertising may not be cost effective; however, if your target market is very tightly defined and you can reach them at little cost it may be worth a try. Test it and see if you get results. If you do, continue the ad. If you don't, try something else.

# Email List

As soon as you set up a website, you should start collecting email addresses from your visitors. Publish a monthly email newsletter, offer a free downloadable report, or give some other enticement to get people to sign up. Now you can build a relationship with them, by providing good information and special offers through your emails.

Never add anyone to the list unless they have given explicit permission. You do not have permission to add someone to your list just because they gave you their card and their card includes an email address. The best thing to do when building a list is to use a email list service that provides confirmed opt-in. That means that when someone signs up for the list they get an email with a link they have to click on to verify that they want to sign up. With confirmed opt-in, you are less likely to have problems with people accusing you of spamming them. The service I use is at http://MailYourCustomers.com/.

# Free Publicity

Publicity is a great marketing method for the Solopreneur. An article about you, or even a mention of your business, in the local newspaper, or a television interview, can have a dramatic impact. I've seen the results with my own publicity efforts and publicity I've gotten for clients. It really works, and you can get publicity.

A press release tells the media about something which has happened or is about to happen. Find a *hook* to interest the editor or reporter. Sending a press release saying that Sallie Jo Johnson has started a business probably won't get you results. But if you were the first person to start a business selling products for left-handers, you could send a press release announcing the formation of a business to solve the unique problems faced by lefties. Most right-handed people don't even realize the problems that lefties face in a right-handed world. That's a hook for a story and may catch the interest of editors.

You can also get publicity by connecting with reporters on social media. I was featured in a story in the *Houston Chronicle* because I responded to a query on Twitter. Or subscribe to the free Help a Reporter

Out (HARO) service at http://HelpAReporter.com/. Reporters post requests for experts to help them with stories. You may be able to get a mention in a small newsletter or even a major outlet such as *The Wall Street Journal.*

Remember when contacting journalists that newspapers, magazines, radio and TV are not there to publicize your business. They are there to inform and entertain their readers, listeners and viewers, and they don't print everything that is sent to them. You have to show them why this is important to their audiences.

## Networking

One of the best ways to get business is by word of mouth. It stands to reason, therefore, that the more people you meet and get to know, the more word of mouth you will generate and the more business you can do. It is not productive, though, to go to so many networking meetings that you have no time for anything else. Networking is one way to get the word out, so use it along with other methods.

Don't rely only on formal networking events. Talk to everyone about what you do. Strike up conversations while you are in line at the bank, shopping at the mall, or anywhere you see other people. You never know if the person you meet is a potential customer. Even if they are not, it is likely that they know someone who is in need of what you offer.

It is also important to establish your own support network. Solo-preneuring can be lonely. Even if you are in contact with customers and suppliers each day, it's not the same as having a group of co-workers on whom you can rely. The members of your network can supply the camaraderie and support that you may miss when you are on your own.

It is important to have others with whom you can share your triumphs and your setbacks. Someone to call on when you need advice, someone you can warn away from making the mistakes you made, and sometimes just a shoulder to cry on.

Who should be in your network? Other Solo-preneurs, especially those in related fields. If you are an accountant, it may benefit you to network with an insurance agent. You may both have the same target market and, since you are not in direct competition, you may be able to refer clients to each other.

It is important that, however you use your network, it does not become one-sided. If you are always asking for help, but not supporting others, you will not be welcome long. And if you are the one doing all the helping, it will be hard for you to see what you get out of the arrangement. To paraphrase a famous quote, ask not what your network can do for you, ask what you and your network can do for each other!

## Borrow Customers to Build Your Business

When you are looking for new customers go where they already are: someone else's business.

Whether your business is established or just starting out, you probably want to find more customers. One great way to get new customers is to borrow them.

Who would let your borrow their customers? Someone who would benefit from their customers doing business with you. Here are just a few examples:

Let someone else sell your products to their customers. I have sold thousands of books through Amazon.com. They have millions of customers, and some of them buy my books.

Amazon has a program called Advantage that almost anyone can use to sell books, audio CDs, DVDs and other products. Even if other retailers do not have programs as accessible as Advantage, you may be able to get your products into their stores, catalogs and web sites.

You can also sell ebooks for Amazon Kindle. Amazon has lots of other ways you can partner with them to make money. For example, you can sell just about any product in the Amazon Marketplace, and even have Amazon ship the orders to customers by using the Fulfillment by Amazon program.

To learn more about how to work with Amazon, go to Amazon.com, scroll down to the bottom of the page, and look for the links headed Make Money with Us.

Once you have an ebook published on Kindle, consider offering it in other market places, such as the Apple store, Barnes & Noble, Smashwords and others. Although you will probably not make as many sales in those stores as on Amazon, once you have a book done, adding it to other stores is fairly simple. (The easy way: Upload it to Smashwords or Draft2Digital and let them get it listed on lots of ebook sites, including Apple.)

Don't forget about eBay, etsy and other sites that put your products in front of their audience.

Udemy.com, Skillfeed.com and other sites will host video courses you create. They sell them to their customers, and send you a portion of the money as much as 97% in some cases.

You can also use an affiliate program or other referral marketing to encourage other marketers to sell your products.

Joint ventures are another way to reach a broader audience. Create a product or service, or market your existing products and services, with someone who is not a direct competitor but sells to a similar market as you.

You could each refer clients to each other, share the cost of a direct mail campaign or newsletter sent to all of your clients or a purchased list of prospects, co-sponsor an event such as a seminar, etc.

You could create a joint venture with businesses in complementary fields that might be as simple as linking to each other's web sites or including fliers for the other business in mailings to your customers.

Get someone else to promote your event to their audience. I have presented seminars and classes through colleges and other organizations. They provide a place, put my program in their catalog, and handle registrations. I show up, teach the class and get paid.

When you are looking for new customers go where they already are—someone else's business.

# CHAPTER 21

# Time and Money

This chapter is all about making the most of your most valuable resource: your time. You only have 24 hours in every day, and once they are gone you cannot get them back. Here are some ideas on using your time profitably.

## The High ROI Hour

If you were to write down all of the things you do in a typical day, what might that list look like? You would probably be surprised to realize how much time you spend on tasks that do not make money for you. For example, in a typical day you might spend one hour on email, two hours on client work, one hour on invoicing and bookkeeping, one hour on the telephone, one hour on social networking and other online activities, and the other two hours...well, who knows where they went.

Based on that list, two hours were spent on actual paying work. The rest was administrative, overhead and wasted time. Although some of those other tasks are necessary (It doesn't pay to do the work if you do not invoice and get paid for it.) it may be possible to have them done by someone other than you. Or you may be able to set up a more efficient system so you spend less time on those tasks.

**Here is the really important part:**

**Ask yourself what you could be doing that would increase your revenues and profits.**

Start scheduling one hour each day to be your "ROI Hour." ROI stands for "return on investment" and this is where you focus on tasks with a high return on the time and money you invest in them.

You may think you do not have the time, but somehow you find the time for the stuff that isn't adding to your bottom line. You need to make time for the tasks that will make you more profitable. These tasks might include:

- Follow up on leads that will bring in new business.

- Create products to generate ongoing passive income.
- Implement an affiliate program to reward people who sell your products and services.
- Identify and recruit affiliates who are a good fit for your program.
- Put a product or affiliate link or two on a high-traffic page.
- Create content to promote your product, service, business or website, then syndicate it to other sites.
- Set up an email list and autoresponder series to stay in touch with people who visited your site.
- List your products on a high-traffic site such as Amazon.com so more customers find-and buy-them.
- Distribute a press release about your business.
- Add upsells or product suggestions to your website or shopping cart.

These will not all be right for your business, and some will be better than others. For example, following up on leads to bring in new business may get some dollars coming in the door right now, but that is a one-time event. To earn more, you have to do it again.

Some of these will take a bit of work to set up, then just a little ongoing maintenance. To sell physical products on sites such as Amazon.com you will have to set up an account and add your product information, then ship product to them from time to time (perhaps monthly or quarterly). In return, you can receive some nice monthly paychecks.

Other ideas on the list may pay you back for months or years after you do them once. For example, by adding an affiliate link to one page of my site I generated nearly $100 a month for months. That may not sound like much, but it took all of 10 minutes to do something that has paid off with (so far) hundreds of dollars in pure profit. Does earning well over $2000 an hour sound good to you? That is what I call "high ROI."

Also think about things that will free up your time and enable you to be more profitable in the long term. For example, you might spend time documenting how you do certain tasks so that you can easily turn those tasks over to a staff member or virtual assistant. That will give you more ROI Hours to make your business even more profitable.

## How to Get Started

First, identify some high ROI tasks you can do. Look through the above list for ideas, or come up with one or more of your own. Next, block out an hour each day on your calendar to work on your high ROI tasks. Choose a time when you are at your best. Treat the appointment as seriously as you would a meeting with an important client.

Keep looking for more high ROI opportunities, then implement them. Do not limit yourself to one high ROI hour per day. Use some of your increased earnings to outsource some of your current tasks and use the time you free up for more high ROI actions.

# Time Management: Making the Best Use of a Limited Resource

We each have the same amount of time in every day, week, month and year, but have you noticed how much more some people get out of them than others? They are not superhuman. They've just realized a few basic facts about managing their time and making the most of it.

### Three Secrets to Managing Time: Organization, Organization, Organization!

A place for everything and everything in its place may sound trite, but when you've just spent two hours trying to locate a piece of paper that wasn't filed, it seems not only true but profound.

If your office and files are organized, you may save hours that you currently spend trying to find things you've misplaced. Your organization system doesn't have to be sophisticated or fancy, it just has to work. Try buying some expandable files or large envelopes, labeling them by category, and dropping receipts and other papers in each file. I use one for tax information (such as receipts), one for things to do (such as bills to pay and letters to answer), one for things I need to read (magazines and newsletters) and so on. I handle the things to do daily, file the tax information monthly, and read from the reading file anytime I can work it in.

### Some Other Time Management Tips ...

Keep focused on your goals. A to-do list or daily plan can help.

Spend time to save time. A day spent learning a new software program can save you days or weeks of time later. You will be using the program the right way, and you won't spend all your time fixing mistakes or trying to find things in the manual. Similarly, a day or two spent organizing your records will pay off almost immediately.

Know your rhythms. If you are not a morning person, don't schedule your most challenging work first thing in the day. Do it at your peak work time. If you work best by taking several short breaks during the day, do it. The increase in productivity will make up for the time you spent on a break.

Group tasks. Don't pull out your checkbook every time you get a bill in the mail. Put the bills in one place and pay them all once a week. Answer all of your correspondence at once. Return your phone calls in one block of time. Run all of your out of office errands at once.

Plan tomorrow at the end of today. Take a few minutes at the end of the day to plan your morning activities for the next day. This is great if you are not a morning person, because you won't have to think about what needs to be done, you can just start doing it!

Don't beat yourself up. No one is productive all the time. You can have some down time when you need it. After all, that's one of the reasons you became a Solo-preneur, right?

# CHAPTER 22

# Getting Help

What about those times when you just can't handle it all yourself? Your business is growing quickly and you can't keep up. Or you just got the two biggest orders ever both due the same day. Or a crisis requires that you take some time away from your business to focus on family.

Plan for this type of occurrence before it happens, and think about where you can get help. Consider each of the following:

- Children and other family members
- Other Solo-preneurs in your network
- High school or college students
- Temporary agencies
- Agencies for the differently-abled (such as Goodwill Industries)
- Mailing services and fulfillment houses

When you need someone with specific skills, you may want to think about hiring a Virtual Assistant (VA). Your VA can be located anywhere (that's what makes them "virtual") and you can often hire them for just a few hours a week. You may even hire multiple VAs, each with a different skill set to handle different groups of tasks.

You may want to outsource certain tasks in your business. One of the best days in my business was the day I hired a fulfillment service to ship books to customers. Up until that time, when I got an order I would pull the book, print a label, stuff the book in an envelope and take it to the post office. Ick! By the time I found a service that I wanted to hire, I estimate that I was spending the equivalent of one day a week shipping books. That is not the best use of my time. Watch out for "task creep" where you start spending lots of time doing low-level routine tasks that can easily be done by someone else.

If you need advice about running your business, contact the Small Business Administration, the Service Corps of Retired Executives (SCORE), or your local Chamber of Commerce. They may be able to direct you to a mentor who can help you.

## Making it on Your Own:
## Alone but Not Lonely

One of the problems we all can encounter when Solo-preneuring has to do with the "solo" part. Depending on the kind of work you do, this can be a lonely existence. Even if your work brings you in contact with people often, it's not the same as having a group of co-workers you see everyday. Co-workers who know you and with whom you can share your trials and tribulations, as well as your achievements.

Now, you may be that soul who doesn't need other people and would be perfectly happy to toil away on a desert island, far away from all else. Most of us, however, need some regular contact and the occasional shoulder to cry on.

I have a couple of friends who also function as accountability partners. Each Monday, I send an email listing my plans and goals for the week. The following Monday, I send another email detailing which ones I got done and which I didn't complete. I am pretty self-disciplined, but it helps to know that someone else is paying attention to what I do (and what I don't do).

Get to know other Solo-preneurs by joining local business and networking organizations. Assemble your own group of Solo-preneurs, and get together for breakfast every week or two. Or, if you aren't interested in being part of a formal group, make sure you have a few friends who understand what you are going through, both good and bad. You need to be able to talk to other people who understand the frustrations and joys of being on your own.

Don't wait until you are feeling isolated to start building your network and support group. Join a group or two and attend meetings regularly. Develop a few relationships with other Solo-preneurs, so that you can share your challenges and your accomplishments.

Sometimes when you're facing a difficult situation, just having another person in your situation who will listen to you and let you talk it out helps you find your solution. Other times, your support network can give you good advice on how they handled a problem. And, of course, you may be able to help each other by providing business or referrals to each other.

# CHAPTER 23

# So, What Are You Waiting For?

The best time to start is always now. Stop saying that "someday" you will take charge of your life and do what you have always wanted to do. Get out your calendar and look at every page. Do you see anything labeled "someday"? I didn't think so. "Someday" is a code word for "never."

Don't wait for the kids to go to school, or finish school, or move out. Don't wait for the day when you have more money, or more time, or more whatever. And don't think that you are too young or too old, not smart enough or creative enough, or somehow not good enough to do this. There will always be more to learn and do, so don't think that everything has to be perfect when you start.

You've heard the proverb that "The journey of a thousand miles begins with a single step," right? Take that first step today. The second step will be easier, and each subsequent step will bring you closer to your goals. But you will never get closer until you take that first step.

Choose an action and start. That might be coming up with a name for your business, finding out about licensing and other legal requirements, deciding what products or services you will offer or setting up a workspace. Just choose something and do it. Don't worry about which is the perfect thing to do first—doing anything is better than doing nothing.

If you need more help, visit my website at http://IdeaLady.com/ to learn about the resources I have available.

Send your comments about this book and Solo-preneuring to me at cathy@idealady.com. And I'm always interested in hearing your success stories! If you have become a successful Solo-preneur, drop me a line. I'd love to hear about how you are achieving your dream.

# Resources

## Set Up a Website

Website Hosting
This is the company I recommend for web hosting.
They are inexpensive and provide lots of features
and great support.
www.MyFavoriteWebHost.com

Email List Service
You need to start building an email list as soon as
possible. This is the company I use and recommend.
www.MailYourCustomers.com

Search Engine Help
Learn the secrets of getting highly ranked in the
search engines.
www.SEOSmarts.com

Google Tools

Google provides lots of free resources to help you with your website.

Webmaster Tools - See how Google sees your website, what you can do to improve your search engine rankings and more

www.google.com/webmasters

Analytics - Get detailed information about how many visitors you get to your site, how they got there, what they viewed on your site and more.

www.google.com/analytics

AdSense - Run Google ads on your site and get paid.

www.google.com/adsense


PayPal

Accept payments online with PayPal. They also offer an online shopping cart and a device you can use with your smartphone or tablet to take offline payments through PayPal Here.

www.PayPal.com


e-junkie

Inexpensive shopping cart and digital download delivery

www.e-junkie.com

## Buy and Sell Services

You can find freelancers to do work for you at these sites, or you can offer your services there.

Fiverr.com
What will people do for $5? Write a press release, compose a jingle, do voice over work and more. Quality is highly variable, but I have gotten some amazing work done here for $5 and up.
www.fiverr.com

Upwork.com
Find freelancers to work for you (e.g., writing, technical and other services) or sell your services here.
www.upwork.com

Mturk
Inexpensive help with simple tasks
www.mturk.com

Udemy.com
Enroll in or present your own online courses
www.Udemy.com

# Sell Your Stuff

eBay
Sell your products through online auctions. This is the top site to do it.
www.ebay.com

Half.com
This sister-site of eBay allows you to sell used books, CDs and DVDs. Some folks have started businesses reselling here.
www.half.com

Amazon.com
Amazon offers many ways to make money by selling just about anything, including books and ebooks, your own line of products, services and more. Go to Amazon.com and scroll down the page to "Make Money with Us."
www.amazon.com

etsy.com
Sell your arts and crafts (and related wares) here.
www.etsy.com

# About Cathy Stucker

Cathy Stucker is The Idea Lady. She helps entrepreneurs, professionals, authors and publishers build expert reputations and attract customers with techniques that make marketing easy, inexpensive and fun.

Cathy provides hands-on help through her consulting services, and teaches clients as well as do-it-yourselfers in seminars and teleclasses. She also publishes manuals, special reports, booklets, audio tapes and ebooks with step-by-step instructions anyone can use successfully.

Cathy Stucker has instructed courses for a number of colleges and universities, , and regularly presents seminars for many continuing education programs, community and business organizations.

Cathy is a frequent media guest. In addition to many appearances on Houston-area television programs, she has appeared on radio programs from coast to coast. Cathy has been featured in stories in *The Houston Chronicle, The New York Times, Woman's Day*, the *Associated Press, Woman's World, Black Enterprise,* and many others.

When she is not being written about, Cathy is writing. And she is a prolific author and publisher. Her articles have been published in national magazines and other print and electronic publications. She has created a variety of information products to educate entrepreneurs and others, and one of her publications is in the collection of the George H. W. Bush Presidential Library.

## How Can You Contact Cathy?

For more information about Cathy Stucker, her products and services, visit her web site at http://www.IdeaLady.com. To request a free subscription to her newsletter, IdeaLady Insider, visit http://www.IdeaLady.com/. For more information about her products and services, or to schedule an interview, call her at 281-265-7342. Cathy can be reached via email at cathy@idealady.com.

You can learn more about Cathy at http://ConnectWithCathy.com/.

www.ingramcontent.com/pod-product-compliance
Lightning Source LLC
Chambersburg PA
CBHW060557200326
41521CB00007B/594